NATIVES OF THE FAR NORTH

NATIVES OF THE FAR NORTH

Alaska's Vanishing Culture in the Eye of Edward Sheriff Curtis

➤

BY SHANNON LOWRY
PHOTOS BY EDWARD S. CURTIS

STACKPOLE
BOOKS

Copyright © 1994 by Stackpole Books

Published by
STACKPOLE BOOKS
5067 Ritter Road
Mechanicsburg, PA 17055

Printed in the United States of America

Cover design by Caroline Miller
Map pp. 5–6 by Sandra M. Blair

10 9 8 7 6 5 4 3 2 1

Library of Congress Cataloging-in-Publication Data

Lowry, Shannon.
    Natives of the far North : Alaska's vanishing culture in the eye of Edward Sheriff Curtis / by Shannon Lowry ; photos by Edward S. Curtis.
        p.   cm.
    Includes bibliographical references.
    ISBN 0-8117-1102-1
    1. Inuit—Alaska.   2. Inuit—Alaska—Pictorial works.   3. Yupik Eskimos.   4. Yupik Eskimos—Pictorial works.   5. Curtis, Edward S., 1868–1952.   I. Curtis, Edward S., 1868–1952.   II. Title.
E99.E7L73   1994
979.8'004976—dc20   94-13657
                              CIP

To the Inupiak and Yupik peoples of the Bering Strait,
who teach us to respect life
and the earth.
It is said that to be one with the inua,
or spirit of the animals,
requires patience, grace, and using all of one's senses
to fly with Eagle,
swim with Walrus,
ride Polar Bear to the moon.
May the Eskimo people always dance and sing
for joy's sake
and keep the stories of the Ancient Ones bright
before the fires
of the darkest season of the year.

Contents

Acknowledgments

>

There are many to thank. Sharon Cloud of Chugiak, my dollmaker friend, sister in spirit, granddaughter of a shaman, daughter of the wind, taught me the ways of the eagle and the lessons of her people: to listen with one's heart, to utilize all of one's senses to perceive both the seen and the unseen, to respect the young and old and, above all, the earth, which sustains life—and to always give back more than one takes. These stories are especially for you, Sharon. I also am indebted to Sharon's mother, Lillian Ingram, for transporting me to another time long ago in her stories of Shishmaref, and her family's harrowing early history along the Bering Sea coast.

Gladi Kulp, library assistant and ace sleuth at the Alaska State Library in Juneau, offered much good initial advice on avenues of research regarding Eskimo legends and songs, as well as biographical information on Edward Curtis.

India Spartz, photographs librarian at the Alaska State Library, put me in touch with a treasure trove of Curtis photographs housed at the University of Alaska–Fairbanks and the University of Washington libraries.

The June Metcalfe Collection at the University of Alaska–Fairbanks yielded, among other important artifacts, Curtis's revealing field guide of his 1927 season with the Bering Strait peoples, thanks to the research work of Marge Naylor, library technician II.

Richard H. Engeman, photographs and graphics librarian with the Special Collections and Preservations Division at the University of Washington in Seattle, offered boxes of yellowed newspaper clippings, archived photos from Curtis's excursions to Alaska, and an engaging knowledge of Curtis's life and times.

Micheal Kerls, a helicopter pilot with the Texas Air National Guard who spends his summers flying copters in Alaska, gave me a number of insights into the life of the Yupik people of Nunivak Island. He spent the summer of 1991 taking part in an archeological survey of Nunivak Island with the Bureau of Indian Affairs, and flew the island's oldest elder around the island to identify ancient sites and recount local legends. Alice Smith, a native Nunivak Islander whose grandparents were among those photographed by Curtis in 1927, was a great help to me in identifying early photos and detailing the types of clothing worn by her ancestors.

Ken Pratt, with the Bureau of Indian Affairs, ANCSA Office, and Robert D. Shaw, of the Alaska Office of History and Archeology, graciously lent me their soon-to-be-published paper on a mysterious stone sculpture of a human head that was discovered by the elders of Nunivak Island. Legends surrounding this stone head and others thought to be located at ancient sites around Nunivak Island go back at least five generations among the island's people. According to legend, the stone heads were the juggling balls that belonged to a giant named Mellaarpag.

In August 1986, this stone head was removed from an islet adjacent to Nunivak Island with the consent of the IRA/Traditional Council of Mekoryuk, Alaska. It is now on loan to the Anchorage Museum of History and Art for curation. In considering the hazards associated with spiriting off toys belonging to a giant, it is this author's sincere hope that the stone head will one day soon be returned to its prehistoric place among the Nunivak people.

All of the following individuals also were inspirations to this undertaking: Alaskan photographer George Herben; expatriate Alaskan Janet Pursley; University of Alaska–Anchorage psychologist Susan Johnson; Doug Barry, director of the Pacific Rim Institute; Mike Holloway, head of orthopedic surgery with the Alaska Native Health Service; Alaskan archeologist Chuck Mobley; author Art Davidson; Paul Tiulana, chief of the traditional King Island people; Alaskan poet Ann Chandonnet; Cynthia Wentworth with the U.S. Fish and Wildlife Service in Bethel; *Alaska Magazine*'s senior editor Jill Shepherd; all of the fine folks at the *Anchorage Daily News* who wrote the Pulitzer Prize-winning series "People in Peril"; and author Dorothy Jean Ray, whose epic book, *The*

Eskimos of the Bering Strait, 1650–1898 (Seattle: University of Washington Press, 1975), was perhaps the finest work available on the history of the Eskimo people.

I'd also like to acknowledge the work of author Barbara A. Davis, whose decade of efforts resulted in the most definitive personal history of the photographer to date, *Edward S. Curtis: The Life and Times of a Shadow Catcher* (San Francisco: Chronicle Books, 1985). I highly recommend Dorothy Jean Ray's book to those who want to learn more about the Bering Strait peoples, and Barbara Davis's book for those bitten by the Curtis bug.

Clive Ponting of Wales, who wrote *The Green History of the World*, must be thanked for pointing out that the last ecologically stable group of people to inhabit the earth were hunters and gatherers such as the Inuit people; and William McNeill, author of *The Rise of the West*, provided an excellent overview of the contributions of ancient peoples to global history during his February 1993 lecture at Southwestern University's Brown Symposium XV, "Macrohistory: New Visions of the World." Special thanks to Dr. Weldon Crowley, history professor at Southwestern University and coordinator of Brown Symposium XV, who suffered my endless stream of questions about ancient history during the winter and spring of 1992–93.

I am particularly blessed by the friendship extended to me by Mary Stachelrodt, a traditional spiritual healer originally from Nelson Island, Alaska, whose fierce work to help overcome alcoholism and drug addiction among the Alaska native peoples is of inestimable value. Dorothy Larson of the Alaska Federation of Natives shared much with me about traditional family values and the crucial link between subsistence and the perpetuation of native culture.

Native artists John Kailukiak, a traditional Yupik maskmaker who lives in Toksook Bay;

Charley Post; James Schoppert; Harvey Pootogooluk of Shishmaref; Rick Seeganna; Joseph Senungetuk of Wales; Larry Ahvakana, who grew up in Barrow and Anchorage; and Seattle artist Lawrence Beck all served as my able and wise initiators into the world of native masks. I'd also like to acknowledge the efforts of the staff of the Native Arts Center at the University of Alaska–Fairbanks, who organized the first Alaska native maskmaking workshop in 1978 and have done much to encourage, elevate, and illuminate this highly sophisticated and once nearly lost art form.

Finally, I'd like to thank the late Edward Sheriff Curtis for lighting a fire on the distant horizon, a fire so big it ignited the long Alaskan winter nights and set me to wandering places I never dreamed I would reach.

EDWARD SHERIFF CURTIS

The Man behind the Camera

➤

Tucked into the high stacks of museum archives across the country are twenty leather-bound volumes of stunning photographs and fluid text collectively called *The North American Indian.* These twenty books represent thirty years in the life of Edward Sheriff Curtis.

Over the course of the three decades it took Curtis to complete *The North American Indian,* from the turn of the century to 1930, he took more than forty thousand photographs of native people throughout the western United States, Canada, and Alaska. His images of Comanche chiefs and Hopi children, Eskimo shamans and Cree women convey a deep trust between Curtis and the people he photographed. He wrote four books and supervised sixteen others, collected more than 350 traditional American Indian legends, and made more than ten thousand recordings of Indian speech and music.

Curtis's works are at once objects of collection and of derision. A complete set of *The North American Indian* can now command up to $100,000, yet many critics revile his photographs as deceptive, contending that Curtis set

up his subjects with studio-like methods but presented the shots as candid. His proponents argue that he had no intention of deliberately misleading the public but was simply using the photographic techniques with which he was most familiar.

Still, Curtis was not above deception when it was to his advantage. The very beginning of his career was based on a deceit that cost him his relationship with his brother Asahel. Evidence suggests that although he said he had first visited Alaska in 1897 to photograph the Klondike gold rush, it was probably Asahel, a fine photographer in his own right, who made that arduous trip to Skagway and over the mountain pass into Canada. The story and photographs Asahel shipped back to Edward appeared in the March 1898 edition of *The Century Illustrated* as "The Rush to the Klondike over the Mountain Passes with Photos and Text by Edward S. Curtis."

When Asahel returned from the dangerous Klondike trip to the Curtis portrait studio in Seattle and discovered that Edward had appropriated his material, he was so incensed that he broke with the family business. The two broth-

ers never again spoke. Their children, who grew up in Seattle, did not know one another.

The Klondike piece was the first article Edward Curtis had published, and he profited from the deception. His supposed work in Alaska in 1897, along with three legitimate portraits of Seattle Indians, earned him the respect of George Bird Grinnell, editor of *Forest and Stream* magazine in New York City and a noted early authority on North American Indians.

One day in 1898, Curtis was photographing Mount Rainier when he happened upon a lost climbing party, whose members fortuitously included Grinnell and conservationist Gifford Pinchot. Curtis, a handsome, somewhat mysterious-looking westerner who wore fringed buckskins and a wide-brimmed felt hat, led the party down the slopes. Grinnell invited Curtis to be one of the official photographers on an extensive scientific expedition to Alaska in 1899, financed by railroad tycoon Edward Harriman.

Curtis sailed from Seattle in May 1899 with the illustrious Harriman Expedition, a floating university of 126 scientists, naturalists, and artists. The two-month voyage covered nine thousand miles and uncovered a wealth of new information about Alaskan flora and fauna, geology, climate, native populations, and geography.

Curtis's first trip to Alaska was just a few decades after the railroads opened the vast expanse of the Wild West to civilization. The Indian Wars of the 1870s had left blood and scars and bitterness on both the land and its indigenous peoples. The consensus among white settlers in popular accounts was that Indians were little more than illiterate, dirty savages. In those days, even the most respected white men in America, including Theodore Roosevelt, considered the white race far superior to that of American Indians.

Curtis went to Alaska in 1899 with the same set of prejudices, but in the Far North, he found for the first time intact and relatively untouched tribes, still going about their lives as they had for at least eleven thousand years. As prospectors entered Alaska in search of gold, Curtis realized he had but a small window of time to create a permanent record of those peoples who, because of geographic isolation, had not yet faced the onslaught of western civilization. He sensed that the American Indian way of life was unraveling in his lifetime.

Months after the Harriman Expedition, Curtis accompanied Grinnell to Montana to the Piegan reservation to witness the Blackfeet Indian gathering for the sacred annual Sun Dance. It was here, experiencing a ritual that was "wild, terrifying and elaborately mystifying," that Curtis discovered his life's own true path. He told Grinnell he wanted to visit all the tribes in the West to record their histories and languages, and to photograph them.

Curtis intended to engage the viewer's feelings of respect for a culture that had been undermined by the relentless press of European immigrants. He wanted his work to provide a comprehensive record of pictures and descriptions so that the Indian could not "by future generations be forgotten, misconstrued, too much idealized or too greatly underestimated."

The photos also subtly chronicle Curtis's personal transformation over the years from an Anglo photographer on a professional mission to one who became native to this country—in essence, Indian—in thought, beliefs, and nomadic lifestyle. His three decades among the American Indians led him to a dramatically different understanding of the sacredness of life. The ways of the native peoples transformed Curtis and tested his inner spiritual strength and his will to survive. He learned far more from them than he could have hoped to give back. And he found a sense of belonging among the

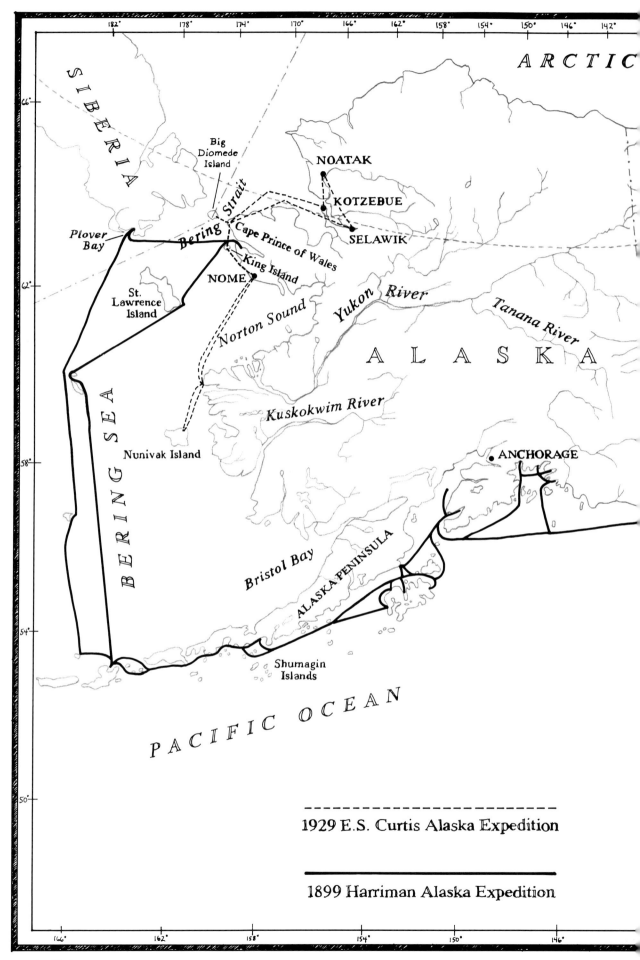

ARCTIC

SIBERIA

Big
Diomede
Island

Bering Strait

Plover
Bay

Cape Prince of Wales

NOATAK

KOTZEBUE

SELAWIK

King Island

NOME

St.
Lawrence
Island

Norton Sound

Yukon River

Tanana River

ALASKA

BERING SEA

Kuskokwim River

Nunivak Island

ANCHORAGE

Bristol Bay

ALASKA PENINSULA

Shumagin
Islands

PACIFIC OCEAN

- -

1929 E.S. Curtis Alaska Expedition

1899 Harriman Alaska Expedition

Sandra Blair

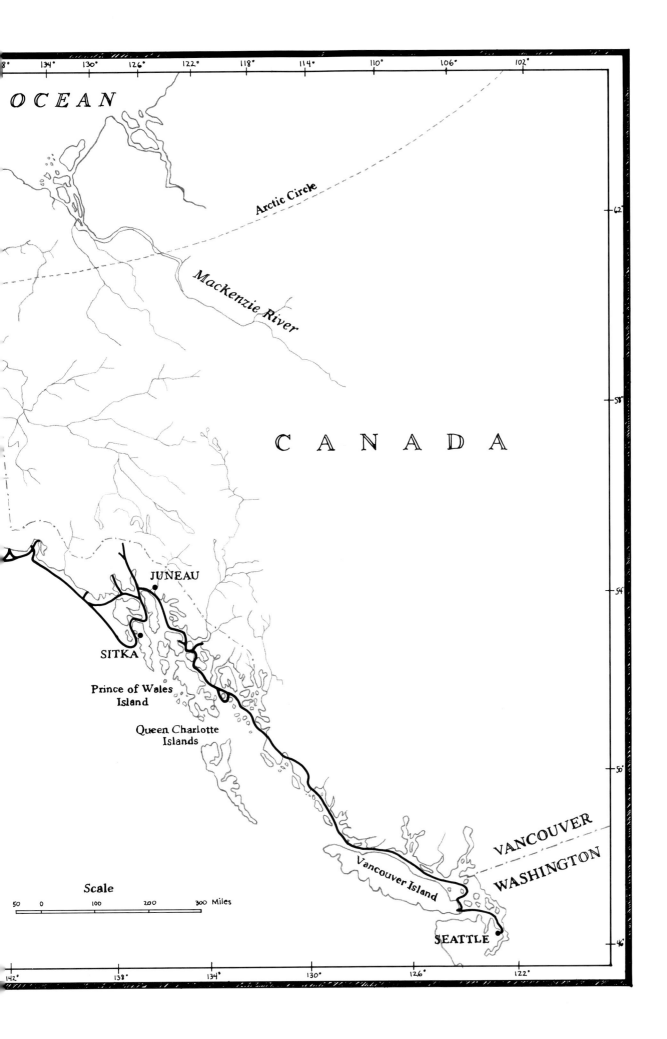

OCEAN

Arctic Circle

Mackenzie River

CANADA

JUNEAU

SITKA

Prince of Wales
Island

Queen Charlotte
Islands

VANCOUVER

WASHINGTON

Vancouver Island

Scale

50   0   100   200   300 Miles

SEATTLE

Eskimo and the Indian that he seemed incapable of attaining among his own kind.

"Ever since the days of Columbus," he wrote, "the assertion has been made repeatedly that the Indian has no religion and no code of ethics, chiefly for the reason that in his primitive state he recognizes no supreme God. Yet the fact remains that no people have a more elaborate religious system than the aborigines, and none are more devout in their performance of the duties connected therewith. There is scarcely an act in an Indian's life that does not involve some ceremonial performance or is not in itself a religious act, sometimes so complicated that much time and study are required to grasp even a part of its real meaning, for his myriad deities must all be propitiated lest some dire disaster befall him."

In a 1907 lecture at the University of Washington, Curtis passed off the difficulty of his fieldwork in a few brief sentences yet lingered over his own deepening immersion into Indian life: "To the oft-asked question, 'What camera or lens do you use?' I can only reply, 'I couldn't tell to save my soul—it is enough for me to know that I have something which will make pictures and that it is in working order. And, as to chemicals, I have almost forgotten that they are a necessary part of photography. . . . But for every hour of misery, I could tell you one which is a joy, and for every page of these trials I could write you countless ones of the beauties of Indian land and Indian life.'"

Over time, Curtis alienated the eastern establishment, who largely financed his work, by his unorthodox lifestyle and his conviction that the white way, the Christian way of life, was in no way superior to that of the Indians.

In the May 1912 issue of *The Hampton Magazine* ("The Vanishing Red Man: Inhumanity of the White Man toward the North American Indian Discussed by Edward S. Curtis"), Curtis dived headlong into a highly opinionated and controversial discourse on what he considered the biggest mistake European immigrants had made in his era. According to Curtis, the immigrants had chosen a misguided course in their prohibition of intermarriage with American Indians. By their insistence on keeping the races separate, the immigrants had shortchanged themselves: "We might have made of him [the Indian] a racial ingredient of inestimable value to us and to the world, had we not instead, shortsightedly, sentenced him to death, and directly or indirectly, put this sentence into operation. We debauched, infected and slaughtered him. Had we preserved him, and accepted from him those fine qualities of blood and brain which he would, in that case, certainly have given us, the American of now and of days to come would inevitably have been a finer, a more distinctive race. It is our fate to build ourselves of blended blood, yet we scornfully refused one of the best strains offered, accepting instead much which is inferior from the European races which have formed a part of our enormous immigration, and which we have welcomed with open arms."

In this same article, Curtis discussed the debilitating effects of alcohol on the Indian race, the federal government's repossession of Indian lands, and the Indians' growing mistrust of American policies. Further, he suggested that white men and women might learn valuable lessons from natives with advantage to American morals and child-rearing practices.

These were not the words of an objective ethnographer or a racist; these were the words of a white man who had long embraced the visions and values of a race that stood in stark contrast and often in direct opposition to those of his own culture.

After three decades of work in difficult conditions among the American Indian tribes of the lower forty-eight and Canada, Curtis returned to Alaska's Bering Sea coast in 1927 to finish the final volume, number 20, in his series.

On his first trip to Alaska at the age of thirty-one, Curtis had traveled in style as a member of the Harriman Expedition. When he reached Nome in 1927, he was fifty-nine years old. A recurring injury to his hip had left him barely able to walk. He was struggling financially, shabbily dressed, and in pain. This trip north held none of the fanfare or great promise of his first voyage. The romantic attraction of the Wild West and the once fashionable interest in his work, along with the financial patronage of J. Pierpont Morgan, had been exhausted. Curtis's daughter, Beth, who traveled with him part of the way on this final research trip, thought when she left him in Nome that it might be the last time she would see her father alive.

Curtis took with him his assistant, Steward C. Eastwood, who reportedly possessed a photographic memory and was an excellent linguist. They set out in a leaky boat named the *Jewel Guard,* having hired its former owner, a native, as a guide.

Despite his deteriorating health, Curtis delighted in the people he met on Nunivak Island that summer: "Think of it. At last, and for the first time in my thirty years work . . . I have found a place where no missionary has worked," Curtis wrote cheerfully in his 1927 field journal.

SEALERS' CAMP, YAKUTAT BAY. E. S. CURTIS, 1899, SPECIAL COLLECTIONS DIVISION, UNIVERSITY OF WASHINGTON LIBRARIES, NEGATIVE NO. NA 2101. _____

DESERTED VILLAGE, CAPE FOX. *It is likely that the village was not deserted, as Curtis's original caption suggests, but rather the people were off at fish camp elsewhere.* E. S. CURTIS, 1899, HARRIMAN ALASKA EXPEDITION ALBUM, SPECIAL COLLECTIONS DIVISION, UNIVERSITY OF WASHINGTON LIBRARIES, NEGATIVE NO. NA 2129.

"I hesitate to mention it for fear some over-zealous sky pilot will feel called upon to labor these unspoiled people. The Native here are perhaps the most primitive on the North American continent. They are so happy and contented that it would be a crime to bring upsetting discord to them. Should any misguided missionary start for this island, I trust the sea will do its duty."

Curtis confined his public dismay over the natives' plight to his brief introduction to volume 20. "While many of the Eskimo visited and studied by the writer still retain much of their hardihood," he wrote, "they appear to have lost not a little of the vigor observed during his study of the coast Eskimo 20 years ago. As among so many primitive people, contact with whites and the acquirement of their diseases have worked a tragic change during this period. A notable exception was found in the Natives of Nunivak Island, whose almost total freedom from Caucasian contact has thus far been their salvation. . . . In all the author's experience among Indians and Eskimo he never knew a happier or more thoroughly honest and self-reliant people."

Curtis ran up one red flag in his introduction, regarding the Eskimos' ready adaptability, "even to the extent of desiring at once to assimilate, at least outwardly, the manners of white men about him." He continued: "In this respect, the Eskimo stands in strong contrast to the average Indian, whose attitude, evidently because of the distrust he has learned to engender toward the whites, is that of contempt."

In Curtis's formal writings on the Eskimo people in volume 20, he chose to ignore the effects of Christianity and white culture. In stark contrast, in his private diary, which he titled "A Rambling Log of the Field Season of the Summer of 1927," Curtis's anger over his brushes with Christian missionaries and their impact on native culture is set down in fiery detail.

"The natives of the Kotzebue region are cursed with a particular vicious brand of missionary, some sort of branch of the Friends," Curtis wrote privately. "All natives who do not belong to and help support the missionary organization are termed Devil People. All those belonging to the organization must give 10 percent of all their intake to support the missions in China; so the missionary boss says. It matters not whether the native is trapping, hunting, or working as a laborer for the mining companies, he must give up one-tenth of it to this bunch of grafters. If the money was used to care for the local natives who were in distress such tithe collecting could be looked upon with favor, but as

CHIEF'S HOUSE, CAPE FOX. E. S. CURTIS, 1899, HARRIMAN ALASKA EXPEDITION ALBUM, SPECIAL COLLECTIONS DIVISION, UNIVERSITY OF WASHINGTON LIBRARIES, NEGATIVE NO. NA 2132.

none of it is so used, it is just rank graft. So high-handed is this organization that it will not permit natives to extend personal aid to any who may not be members of the Church. This extends so far that members of a family are not allowed to aid relatives unless they be Christ People and all this in the name of Christ."

When Curtis and Eastwood went to visit an old informant upriver from the village, whom the missionary had deemed a "Devil Man," Curtis wrote, "This man has been driven from the village by the missionaries owing to his refusal to be a Christian. The old man is a cripple and a most pathetic case. Missionary will not allow relatives to assist him in any way."

He also reveals in his diary his disapproval of a group of National Museum archeologists he encountered in the Bering Sea islands. They were, in his view, headhunters and grave robbers. And even though Curtis reluctantly agreed, as was the custom and traveler's code of the North, to transport the archeologists to a nearby location, his native pilot warned him that nothing good would come of having looted skulls on board. Later on, when a storm brought high seas and ice to the deck of the *Jewel Guard,* Curtis blamed the bad-luck voyage on the headhunters, saying they had aroused the spirits of the dead whose skulls he had transported.

The expedition pressed on to King Island, where the Eskimos lived part of each year in huts on twenty-foot stilts set against the cliffs. Curtis and Eastwood collected folk tales among the people there and on Little Diomede Island. With the brief summer coming to a close, the trio landed in Kotzebue Sound, where they planned to spend three weeks. The natives had already pulled their skin boats out of the water for winter. On the return trip to Nome, Curtis and his party ran into the season's first blizzard, and they worked round the clock to pump out their leaking hull and keep the decks free of ice. When they finally reached Nome, they learned that the last wireless from the North had announced them lost in the blizzard.

"My hunch was that we had about one chance in a thousand," Curtis wrote. "One nice thing about such situations is that the suspense is short lived. You either make it or you don't."

Curtis sailed back to Seattle on the SS *Alemeda,* arriving on Sunday, October 9, and proceeded straight to the station to board a train to Los Angeles. The police arrested him on the platform. He was taken to the county jail and locked up. His ex-wife, Clara, had signed an affidavit alleging his failure to pay $4,500 in alimony for the past seven years.

Curtis posted bond and was released. He made three appearances in court; his weary demeanor and stubborn attitude were duly reported in the *Seattle Post-Intelligencer.* No doubt to the great chagrin of the eastern upper crust, the newspaper also described him as an international character, "friend of Theodore Roosevelt, and associate of the late J. Pierpont Morgan." He was berated in court for refusing to provide for a minor child.

Curtis claimed he had no money and would receive no royalties from *The North American Indian* since the work was being completed at a deficit. The incredulous judge asked him why he was doing it.

Curtis dissolved into tears. "Your Honor," he said, "it was my job. The only thing I could do that was worth doing. A sort of life's work. I was duty-bound to finish it. Some of the subscribers had paid for the whole series in advance."

The case apparently was dismissed when neither party could produce the original alimony decree. No decision was ever published.

UKOWUHHUH, HOOPER BAY. E. S. CURTIS, SPECIAL COLLECTIONS DIVISION, UNIVERSITY OF WASHINGTON LIBRARIES, NEGATIVE NO. NA 2011.

Curtis finally caught the train and limped home to Los Angeles, where he managed to finish his monumental work. "Great is the satisfaction the writer enjoys when he can at last say to all those whose faith has been unbounded, 'It is finished,'" he concluded in his introduction to volume 20. The Alaska volume is credited by critics as being the best written and photographed of the entire collection. It was as if every field technique and photographic method he had learned along the way had culminated in this final effort.

Curtis's hip had so deteriorated by then that he was seeing three doctors and wore a brace to ease the strain. In 1930 the last two volumes were published simultaneously. No reviews of the work were published. By this time, Curtis had disappeared from view. One account places him in Denver from 1930 to 1932, where he reportedly suffered a breakdown, was hospitalized for a time, and was under the care of a doctor.

Though he had steadfastly corresponded with friends and was a skilled and thoughtful letter writer, none of his closest associates heard from him for years. Finally, he penned a note to Bella da Costa Greene, who had been J. Pierpont Morgan's assistant before Morgan's death. She was in charge of the Morgan Library.

"Following my season in the Arctic collecting final materials for volume 20, I suffered a complete physical breakdown and for two years was about a 99 percent loss," he wrote to her. "Ill health and uncertainty as to how I was to solve

PLOVER BAY ESKIMOS (SIBERIAN FAMILY GROUP).

E. S. Curtis, 1899, Harriman Alaska Expedition Album, Special Collections Division, University of Washington Libraries, Negative No. NA 2109.

the problem of the future brought about a period of depression which about crushed me. I could not write to my friends; no one wants to listen to the wail of lost souls, or to the down and outers. I am again writing and hoping that I may do something worth while."

The librarian never replied, but a note filed by her secretary indicates that the Morgan family's patience had been strained over finances long before the end of the project. According to the secretary's note, Curtis had written hoping only to open another avenue of funding through J. Pierpont's son, Jack.

The North American Indian Corporation, whose primary stockholders were the Morgan family, liquidated its assets and in 1935 sold the materials for *The North American Indian* to a rare-book dealer in Boston. The Charles Lauriat company bought nineteen unsold sets of books, thousands of photographic prints, the original

HOOPER BAY HOMES. E. S. Curtis, Special Collections Division, University of Washington Libraries, Negative No. NA 2009.

handmade copper gravure plates, and all copyrights for the paltry sum of $1,000 plus future royalties. The original cost of the copper gravure plates alone had been nearly $100,000.

Curtis's original glass-plate negatives, which had been stored for many years in the Morgan Library basement, were never shipped to Lauriat. Later, during World War II, they would be parceled off as junk and many of them would be destroyed. Lauriat found buyers for his 19 complete sets and assembled 50 more, supplementing the unbound material with new prints on different paper to bring the total number of sets marketed to 291. But Lauriat, in the end, had no better luck marketing Indian books, and the collection wound up in his basement.

SEALERS' CAMP, GLACIER BAY. E. S. Curtis, 1899, Special Collections Division, University of Washington Libraries, Negative No. NA 2094. _____

Meanwhile, Curtis had regained some of his strength and was researching gold mining, which had been a hobby for much of his adult life. Yet his mind frequently crossed into that other world where he had wandered for so long. "In my sleep, I find myself building whole paragraphs in Indian words, which in my normal hours I have quite forgotten," he wrote to a friend in 1938. "In other cases, I am working out statements, thoughts, names, locations, which are unknown to me. Perhaps it is the worry and pain which causes the strange wanderings of my brain in the sleeping hours."

He eventually invested in several mining ventures around Colfax, California, where he spent many summers, but nothing ever came of

his quest for gold. Occasionally he would take off in his beat-up car and disappear for weeks. People in small California towns sometimes mistook him for Buffalo Bill; apparently he didn't correct their error. He tried to work on several articles for publication but never managed to finish them.

In his late sixties, he developed severe stomach problems that kept him in bed. He rallied to travel to South Dakota, where he worked on *The Plainsman,* a film starring Gary Cooper. Set in the Badlands, where Curtis had lived among Red Hawk and his men thirty years before, the movie employed hundreds of Rosebud Sioux and Cheyenne as extras.

Curtis also did a series of blue-tone still publicity photos for the film *The Ten Commandments.* In much of Indian legend, blue is the color of the transitional phase one passes through when entering and leaving the spirit world.

Curtis retired in the late 1940s to a small farm owned by his daughter and her husband in Whittier, California. He died of a heart attack in Los Angeles on October 19, 1952. A brief obituary in *The New York Times* noted that he was an authority on the North American Indian and a photographer.

⟩

In recent years Curtis has been criticized for setting up his shots and for retouching photographs and using wigs and costuming, but he was by profession a studio portrait photographer accustomed to designing and enhancing his shots.

Curtis himself referred to his work as Art-Science. It is in the crack between these two genres that his work seems to have fallen. In this age of microspecialists, the critics who have taken notice have rapped Curtis for not focusing on one field and for romanticizing American Indians. One reviewer said that had Curtis's photographs represented true documents, "they would more closely resemble Dorothea Lange's photographs of migrant workers in the 1930s instead of proud warriors."

In *The Vanishing Race and Other Illusions* (Pantheon, 1982), written to complement a Smithsonian traveling exhibition of Curtis's photography, author Christopher M. Lyman argues that Curtis's work cannot stand as a true reflection of Indian life in the first quarter of the twentieth century. Lyman believes that Curtis was a prisoner of his own time and that his ideas were distorted by racism, racial prejudice, and

DRYING WHALE MEAT, HOOPER BAY. E. S. CURTIS, SPECIAL COLLECTIONS DIVISION, UNIVERSITY OF WASHINGTON LIBRARIES, NEGATIVE NO. NA 2012. _____

ethnocentrism. For all his criticism, though, Lyman is not altogether unappreciative of the project Curtis undertook or of the man who devoted most of his life to photographing the Indians.

In Curtis's images rest the vision of a great romantic imagination. He was far more an artist than a documentary photographer, far more a storyteller than an ethnographer. He in no way tried to feign objectivity in his thousands of photographs, numerous interviews, and copious writings on American Indians.

Curtis's relentless drive to complete his twenty-volume opus wrecked his marriage, damaged his health, and drove him into wild and mostly doomed fund-raising schemes. He died broke, his work out of fashion, his once revered reputation forgotten. During his lifetime, fewer than three hundred sets of *The North American Indian* had been sold, and they were so costly as to be forever relegated to exclusive private collections and rare-book archives.

In 1972 the basement of Charles Lauriat's bookstore yielded Curtis's copper gravure plates. Since then, reprintings have been made of many of the surviving images, and his work is being added to institutional and private collections. Lois Flury and James Flury have been collecting,

MEMBERS OF THE HARRIMAN ALASKA EXPEDITION AT THE "DESERTED VILLAGE," CAPE FOX. *Note: In the background, on the shore, are a number of items expedition members took as "archeological specimens" from the village.* E. S. CURTIS, 1899, HARRIMAN ALASKA EXPEDITION ALBUM, SPECIAL COLLECTIONS DIVISION, UNIVERSITY OF WASHINGTON LIBRARIES, NEGATIVE NO. NA 2030.

buying, and selling vintage Edward S. Curtis images since 1973. According to them, fewer than twenty complete sets of *The North American Indian* have changed hands in the past twenty years; a complete set fetches from $60,000 to $100,000, depending on condition, binding, and the type of paper it is printed on.

Curtis's one great hope for Alaska to remain wild and free rested in his unrealistic notion that its attractions were few. As he steamed north through the Aleutian Islands, Curtis penned in his diary: "Alaska is looked upon as a Pioneer Country, a place where bold and venturesome young men go to start the foundation of wealth, yet, on this ship there is not a half dozen men who are not old timers. This fact tells the story: the gold rush days of the Northland are over. The country is decadent. The white population is less now than it was ten years ago. It was less ten years ago than it was twenty years ago, and barring the unforeseen, it will be still less in ten years from now."

He was wrong. Today's Alaska, bisected by a pipeline and dotted with a number of bustling cities yet still marked by vast regions of uncom-

mon beauty, continues to attract non-natives. But the Eskimo legends and tales Curtis collected in the Far North—and the truth written in the eyes of the people he photographed—will serve to speak to many generations to come.

To travel with Curtis, one has to set aside the trappings and beliefs of white America and the ingrained attitudes of the Judeo-Christian culture. In Alaska, and indeed throughout the West, American Indians believe that the mark of a disciplined man or woman is the ability to still the voices within long enough to sit and listen. To listen to the old tales of the inter-dependence between men and animals and the spirit world that connects them. To listen not with one's head but with one's heart. To suspend a world of science and logic for the feel of the earth beneath one's feet, the songs of the wind, the whispers of the sea.

The pages that follow contain the images and stories of Alaska's first people. Curtis listened to these tales sitting quiet and cross-legged in makeshift fish camps beneath the midnight sun. Sit a spell and listen. Linger among the people Curtis came to understand.

Nunivak Island

CUSTOMS

Life and Death among the Nunivak

➤

Among the Nunivak, village life was made up of small family groups, headed by the father or the grandfather. A newly married man was accepted as a member of his wife's family.

There was no ruling chief of the people, although it was common for an older man, noted for his wisdom, knowledge of spirituality, or hunting ability, to serve as a headman. This *unaiyukah,* or counselor, was an advisor to all those who sought him out. His suggestions were always respected but not always acted upon. Many of the Nunivak legends attest to powerful headmen, however, who became absolute in power and ruled through might and awe.

Sometimes marriage was arranged by the heads of families, but not without the consent of the couple. Usually, a man was free to court and choose the woman he would like to marry, and if she consented to the arrangement, her parents were told the news. Her father would then carry gifts that he deemed of equal worth to his daughter to the men's house, where the men lived during the winter months while they worked together. There he exchanged them for firewood from any of the men present.

Firewood, a scarce commodity, commanded a high price in barter.

The father then held a sweat bath for the men of the village in the men's house. Afterward, the women brought food for their husbands, and the bride placed the food before the man who had chosen her. This simple act constituted the marriage ceremony.

Much has been made of the social custom among the Eskimo of exchanging wives, but on Nunivak, this happened only rarely. Two brothers, raised together and close friends, might marry and exchange wives from time to time. This was done so that paternity would be doubtful and the children would consider themselves brothers and sisters and grow as close in spirit as their fathers.

In fact, adultery by either husband or wife among the Nunivak was considered grounds for divorce. A man could also divorce his wife for failure to perform her chores or for disobedience to her husband or her parents. It was customary for the man to call together all of his wife's relatives and, in her presence, announce the reason why he was leaving. He then returned to the

membership of his own family. If the man failed to provide adequately for the wife, or if she was unable to live in harmony with him, she could divorce her husband by refusing to carry food to him in the men's house.

The birth of a new child was of great significance among the islanders, and for a period of three days after the birth, members of the family could not engage in work and had to remain very quiet. The father then carried barter goods to the men's house and exchanged them for firewood, which he offered for use in a sweat bath. No enemies of the father must be present at the sweat bath, since only goodwill and friendship must exist. Friends of the family brought berries to the home, some of which were scattered on the floor as an offering as they prayed that the newborn child, if a girl, would be a good worker in skins and foodstuffs, or if a boy, would grow to be a good hunter.

The first boy in a family was given his father's name, and the first girl was named for her mother. Successive children were named for relatives. If a couple died with no children, their names, perhaps handed down for generations, died too, unless relatives happened to give those names to their children.

Among the villagers, there was very little violence. Quarrels were settled by combat between the two people involved. No punishment was meted out to anyone who killed another in a fair fight, but an outright murder would be avenged by friends or relatives. The oldest people Curtis and his assistant talked to in 1927 could recall no cases of suicide.

Death was considered a journey, and the dead and dying were dressed as if for distant travel in their best costumes. At night a light was placed before the body. Corpses were removed from the house as soon as possible so that they might proceed at once on the "spirit road." At Cape Etolin, the dead were taken to a burial place outside the village. The body was faced to the east and placed in a wooden grave box on posts, along with food, dishes, and tools. If the body was that of a man, his kayak, sled, spears, and hunting gear were piled atop the box or on the ground beside it. At Nash Harbor, the Eskimo lay the body extended, facing east, in a shallow, oval-shaped grave with food, utensils, and tools, and surrounded by stones.

The spirit of the dead was thought to hover harmlessly, yet visibly, above the village for forty days. The spirit then lost consciousness and awakened to find himself in a land of spirits, many of whom had never been on earth or existed in human form. People who drowned traveled with the wind until their clothing was blown off before they reached this spirit land. The spirits of evil people went to the Eskimo equivalent of hell, a shadowy world far below, heinous beyond mention.

One elderly woman recalled fragments of her childhood days to Curtis; these offer a rare glimpse into Yupik beliefs surrounding death.

She remembered a winter when food was scarce and the people nearly starved. In the spring her relatives took her to a fish camp, where many kayaks stood on racks. The men were working hard to repair their gear and mend nets.

"One day when the women were cutting up walrus, I saw my father land his heavily laden kayak. Women and boys met him to help unload; but one boy ran home crying when my father said that his partner would never return, that he was drowned."

READY FOR THE THROW, NUNIVAK. *Seal hunter.* E. S. Curtis, Special Collections Division, University of Washington Libraries, Negative No. NA 1995. _____

In the men's house, her father told the tale of what had happened. A walrus had come up close to his friend's kayak, and he called to his friend not to harpoon it because the animal was too close. But his friend cast his heavy spear anyway. The angry walrus punched holes with its tusks in the kayak until the boat overturned. The walrus seized the man between its flippers and dragged him screaming beneath the sea. In a short time the walrus broke surface, still holding the man and rubbing its whiskers against the man's face.

Again the walrus dove, and that was the last time her father saw his friend alive.

The battered kayak, still carrying its load of meat, drifted by the fish camp later that day. A few days later, the drowned man's body washed ashore. His relatives stripped off his clothes and boiled them to drive away the evil spirits. Then they put new clothes on him.

"A man tied a child's outfit of parka, mittens and boots on the body, saying, 'When you get up there, give these to my child.' I asked my

NUNIVAK YOUTH. *Reindeer parka with button arm bands.* E. S. Curtis, Special Collections Division, University of Washington Libraries, Negative No. NA 1990. _____

grandmother why he said that, and she replied, 'That man had a child who was drowned. Relatives always give things to a drowned man's body, that he may give them to those, who, drowned, have gone before.' Then I saw others hang things on the body. The people then propped the body up, stiff-legged, with arms outstretched and walking sticks in both hands, as if he were ready to go somewhere. They piled all his clothes and weapons and his kayak about him, and much driftwood. When this was set ablaze, the body melted like a lump of fat. My grandmother said that people worked fast with the body in order to get it started on its journey as soon as possible."

CEREMONIES

Keeping the Fragile Balance

➤

Of the dozens of ceremonial rituals the Nunivak followed, many involved gift giving or trade and were social in nature, while the most important recognized the crucial link between the successful harvest of food and the perpetuation of human life. Ancestors were honored, spirits were appeased, elders were offered foodstuffs and warm clothes, and babies were welcomed. The animals, birds, and fish the islanders hunted were intricately woven into their ceremonies.

The most important Nunivak ceremonies occurred during the winter, the season of *Dunkelloyuh* ("worst of the moon"), when severe storms battered the Bering Sea, daylight hours decreased dramatically, and the islanders were forced indoors.

The Bladder Feast was the most elaborate of these, involving days of preparation, days of ritual, and ending in generous gift giving. The spirits of the dead were thought to be present during the rites and were remembered with food offerings. The feast culminated in a ceremony in which the village men thrust a bladder through a hole in the ice, done to ensure good

hunting and plentiful food throughout the coming year.

The Bladder Feast, according to Nunivak legend, had originated with a childless couple, who always had much food stored away and many furs. They dwelled alone and never saw another person. As time went by, they often thought what it would be like if there were other people. They wondered how to have children. The man thought that if he stored away the bird bladders from his game, he might learn something about his next year's catch, and perhaps something unexpected might happen to them. Winter came, and the man brought out the bladders and inflated them. That night, the couple were startled to see a hand appear in the entrance hole, its fingers outstretched. A voice said, "You must use these five days for your Bladder Feast." The hand disappeared.

Suddenly, six spirits entered the house and then vanished through the walls. The spirits entered again, and placed wild parsnips about the room, and sang and drummed and danced before the fire all night long.

The following night, the spirits came again

and painted the bladders, which were hanging on the wall. The bird bladders changed to seal bladders right before their eyes. The spirits put wild parsnips in all four corners of the room, and went outside to place stones around the house and set the kayak paddles upright. They told the man that while they were busy outside, he was to circle the room in the same manner as the sun makes its path across the sky.

The spirits reentered and brought with them a heavy walrus-clubbing spear, which they set upright beside a stone lamp. The man continued to circle the room. The spirits vanished.

The next night no one came, so the man dared to sleep with his wife. He discovered the following morning that the bladders had changed back to bird bladders. He knew that he had been punished for not obeying the Eskimo law of continence during a ceremony. That night, sitting alone, he saw two old men spirits spring up through the floor and sit facing each other by the entrance hole, where they sang this song:

> My elbows I must use for walking
>   sticks.
> My shoulder blades hump toward my
>   neck.
> My legs are weary.
> But my spirit refuses to become aged.

When the song ended, a woman entered the room, followed by six spirits, who began to dance and sing. As the couple watched, many people suddenly appeared in their home, some naked, some fully clad, singing and swaying their bodies in unison to the rhythm. More people entered, bearing gifts, which they gave away during the songs. Just before dawn, three calls were heard outside, "Luah! Luah! Luah!" One by one, many more people came in with gifts. When these had been distributed to all, everyone in the room except the couple disappeared, leaving all the gifts.

Early in the morning, many men brought in wild parsnips to tie onto the walrus spear. They went outside and gave a long call. The women rushed in, carrying bundles of grass, which they threw at the entrance. The man could see these women spirits very clearly, but they were invisible to his wife.

The two old men spirits by the entrance now wore bird-skin caps. They told the story of an owl who went beneath the sea. After the tale was through, one of the old men went outside and climbed to the roof, where he rattled the smokehole cover so that the people would know day was breaking. The second old man donned his waterproof parka and flopped about the floor, imitating the movements of a seal on the ice. Some of the people smeared soot on their faces. The old man loudly announced from the smokehole, "It is time to go out."

All of the spirit people departed, one of them bearing the stone lamp. The man followed them to a waterhole in the ice, where they thrust all the bladders. The people returned to the house and stripped themselves of all their clothing. Then they rolled through the entrance. Once inside, they disappeared.

After night fell, many women entered to perform a dance. At the end, one of the old spirits spoke to the man: "In the future, you will have children; there will be many people. Every year, when the proper time comes, you must do as you have seen us do. Then you will catch much game. You will never see us again."

The lengthy personal vision that surrounds the origins of the Bladder Feast was perpetuated by the Nunivak Islanders. They held a two-week ritual annually to appease the spirits of the dead, compose new songs, make sacrificial food offerings to the four winds, cast away evil influences, drive the spirits back to spirit land, tell tales of their hunts, wish that the ensuing year will be plentiful in game, and distribute gifts to one another to foster goodwill. Then, as the last song ended, each man would thrust his stick with the bladders beneath the ice. Members of each family group on the thirteenth morning would face the rising sun and sing their ancient hunting song.

A feast was then held, after which two young men would sweep the room. Stories were told of the year's outstanding events. With respect, the hunter's name was never mentioned; rather, the narrator pointed to where he sat. All of the men rushed out at the end, to chase away bad luck. The branches used to sweep the room were thrown into a fire outside. This act ended the Bladder ceremony.

During the next few days, games were played and numerous feasts were held, but first came the "asking ceremony." Sometime during the thirteenth night, a stick was thrown into the men's house. The man who picked up the stick told those present that the objects tied to it represented things that women desired. This wise and no doubt well-coached man would then interpret the meaning of the objects. The men then tied on the stick similar objects, which meant that they would see that the women's wishes were honored.

A grass partition was raised in the men's house on the fourteenth night, with the objects representing what the women had asked for hung over it. While the women sang on their side, the men danced on the other. Afterward, the men hung their gifts over the partition. Then they hung up more gifts, and sang, "No one has taken what I have hung up, so I have promised this gift for ——— [naming the person]." When the woman took this gift, the man was privileged to read her a moral lecture.

An "asking stick" was then given to the

women, and its objects were explained to them. They rushed to the partition with the objects the men desired. Then the men sang while the women danced. Afterward, the women hung their additional gifts on the screen. When the named man took what he had asked for, the woman had the pleasure of reading him a moral lecture.

The fifteenth and final night of this age-old tradition involved group gift giving, with a heaped-up pile of goods distributed to all those present.

➤

During the full moon of January, the Division of Men and Women Feast occurred, which was called the *Anuchchihkiyum* ceremony, or "when women take possession of the men's house."

This ceremony was said to have originated with a couple who lived alone at Cape Mohican. They had a custom of exchanging gifts when feasting or celebrating.

The women in the village would gather outside the men's house on the night of the full moon and cry in unison to the men inside, "Look here! Look here! You are a fine spoonmaker."

The oldest woman then entered first. She carried a dish of berries laced in fat, which she offered to her second cousin or another relative. She requested a gift of some article in return. All the women, from the oldest to the youngest, followed in order with food and requests from relatives. When all were inside, two women, dressed in their best finery, faced one wall and danced while the men accompanied them with drumming and singing. When the dance was finished, the women and the men left the house. The men returned with what had been requested.

Carrying stone lamps, the women reentered and signaled that they were ready. Each man, by descending order of age, brought his gift, entered the room, and danced by the entrance to a tune sung by those still outside. After all were inside, the gifts were presented to the women.

The women then left to gather suitable gifts to present to the men in exchange. While they were gone, the men gathered in a circle, blackened their faces with soot, and traced their spirit marks in the soot. The women, laden with gifts, returned to the room in order of age. After each offered a man her gift, she danced to the singing of the men, and all continued to dance until the last young woman entered.

Perpetuation of good tidings among the people was particularly important during the long, tiresome winter months. The Division of Men and Women Feast honored those unique qualities that male and female members of the community each brought to the feast of life.

➤

In the early spring, when travel is first possible between Nunivak and the mainland, a messenger was sent to invite friendly Eskimo trading partners to the island for the Messenger Feast.

The messenger was sent by the headman with a carved staff about six feet long, decorated with dog skin and two bands of soot and red oxide. The carvings on the staff represented certain people in the trading village to be invited and the specific gifts they should bring. The headman told the messenger what each carving meant. "From this person we ask a kayak load of seal meat and prepared intestines. Let them bring also a sealskin whose hide represents gifts of cloth, whose eyes are cooking pots, and whose penis is ivory. These articles must they furnish."

THE IVORY CARVER, NUNIVAK ISLAND. *Known Christian name: Moses.* E. S. Curtis, Special Collections Division, University of Washington Libraries, Negative No. NA 2008.

Each name mentioned by the headman represented an entire group of people in the village.

The messenger memorized these instructions and blackened his face with soot. Carrying a new smokehole cover and the carved staff, he walked to his sled and departed before daybreak for the other village.

He left his sled before reaching his destination and attempted to enter the village unnoticed. At the men's house, he climbed to the roof and fastened on the new smokehole cover. Carrying the messenger stick, he entered the men's house in blackface and stood in silence before the people. After a long period of silence, the oldest man present called out, "Messenger! Messenger! Messenger!"

He answered, "Messenger! Messenger! Messenger! The headman of my village wishes to see the headman of this village. Let him come with a gift of hair-seal skin."

The messenger sat in the middle of the room on the floor, and a lamp was placed before him. The headman offered him food and water. Before accepting sustenance, the messenger rubbed food on his insteps and poured water on the floor. Afterward, he unwrapped a bundle of sticks the headman gave him to carry and named each person invited to the feast, beginning with the elders. The tally sticks were then thrown into the fire pit. The messenger read from his carved staff the gifts they were to bring. The stick was then hung by the smokehole, so that it too would eventually be consumed by the fire.

In order that the villagers would think well of this invitation, and to create a favorable impression of his own people, the messenger remained for as long as a month in the village, helping the men as much as possible and performing many tasks.

Meanwhile, back in the messenger's village, preparations were in earnest. Men and women gathered in the men's house to practice their songs. For each of the invitation sticks sent out, a new song was created. Masks were made along with many bird and animal carvings of wood.

An agility test to be performed later was practiced with great zeal. A heavy waterlogged timber was suspended horizontally about three feet off the floor. A strong man swung the log while another agile, naked young man leapt over it. Failure to jump at the right moment would send the jumper hurling into the rear wall.

Masks and bird and animal ornaments were suspended near the entrance. Four large drums were made and also hung near the door. Four men were chosen to do the drumming during the festivities. The best singer of the village selected three men and three women singers, who painstakingly rehearsed the new songs to the beat of the drums. The singers learned all the

proper motions and gestures to carry them out to perfection.

In the following days, caps were made of deer, fox, seal, and wolf. A great deal of food was prepared and stored. Finally, the messenger returned home.

Face blackened again, he carried a new carved staff from the invited village, entered his own men's house, and stood silent in the middle of the room. The oldest man yelled "Messenger!" three times, and he answered in kind. He then read from the staff the articles that the visitors had asked of various people of the village. Once this was recited, the stick was broken and the pieces were thrown outside. That night, all the implements made in preparation were brought into the men's house, and a sweat bath was held.

When the visitors approached the next morning, an old man, face blackened and wearing a white parka, went to meet them. He danced them into his home territory. All would stop and

REINDEER, NUNIVAK ISLAND. E. S. Curtis, Special Collections Division, University of Washington Libraries, Negative No. NA 2058.

wait. After a brief ritualistic welcome, hosts and guests alike raced to the men's house. The visitors remained with their sleds until the villagers raised a pole that signified greeting and good trade and then carried food out to their guests.

The headman of the home village then fastened a sealskin to the raised pole and danced about it, signifying that barter was about to begin. The visiting headman took down the sealskin and kept it, replacing it with one of greater value, such as a wolverine or a white fox skin.

The trading proceeded until each group had a large pile of skins. Next the visitors brought out all the articles that had been requested and distributed them in order of age to the hosts. The guests were then invited to various houses.

FAMILY GROUP, NUNIVAK ISLAND. E. S. Curtis, 1928, PCA 49-8, Alaska State Library.

Much singing and dancing followed, along with athletic games. The men wore their masks and caps and danced the visitors into the men's house, where a medicine woman drove away any evil the neighbors might have brought with them. All night and all the next day, the feast continued and the new songs to honor the visitors were sung.

The headmen again exchanged gifts, which were distributed to the villagers in order of age. On the fourth day, all kinds of provisions were brought to the men's house to be given to the visitors, and another feast was held.

A smaller round of gift giving followed on the fifth day, and the dances and new songs were again heralded. Before the villagers departed, a marathon full day and night of singing and dancing was held to acknowledge and strengthen the crucial ties that existed between these trading partners.

➤

The Spring Hunt Ceremony, or consecration of the kayaks, was more serious and personal in nature. It was held the first day after the men reached the spring hunting camp in the season when young seals are born.

Hunters had to be clean of person, wear clean white parkas, and keep their weaponry in perfect order before the stalking of any game took place. During the important seal season, new kayaks or at least new covers were used, and sealers wore new white parkas. After the season, old kayak covers could be stretched over the frame for the purpose of fishing.

Each man made two paddles the length of his arms outstretched, with handles a fist wide. Each painted his animal spirit on his kayak in light blue, a paint made of cupric oxide obtained from the Nelson Islanders. During the days of the ceremony, the men fasted, followed by a feast at night. The owners carried their crafts to the shore and fastened them by lines to upright boat hooks.

Before daybreak on the fourth day, a hunter's wife bathed in urine, rinsed in salt water, then dressed in a new costume. The hunter, meanwhile, entered the men's house with two handfuls of snow. Standing on a grass mat, he rubbed himself from the feet upward with the snow. His wife placed a lighted lamp before him as he dressed in his new clothing. Bearing the lamp and followed by his wife, the hunter went outside to his new kayak, which they circled slowly. The man inserted the lamp into the kayak so that the game might see his kayak and come near. Then the lamp was

quickly withdrawn and set in the snow. The children placed their lamps before their father's.

After placing each weapon and piece of equipment in its proper place, the man carried the kayak to the open water. There, he paddled about slowly, praying for good hunting, plenty of seals, and good weather. He prayed especially that he might catch sea lions and hair seals, which have spirits.

Next, the hunter offered berries to the sea, so that many seals would swim near his kayak, and then he divided the rest of the berries among his sons. When the dish was empty, the man made three clockwise circles in his kayak and then paddled straight out to sea. With this, the spring hunt began. The sons cast their berries into the water as their father departed, offering a prayer that he would kill a seal before the sun set. The wife set out with a sled load of dried fish to distribute to the widows and elders of the village while he was gone.

After killing a hair seal, the hunter skinned it, cut up the meat, and thrust it below deck before paddling for home. To signify his success, he ran to the roof of the men's house, where he slapped each wall with the palms of his hands and yelled his hunting song.

His wife meanwhile changed into her new parka, and the couple took the meat home on a sled. The man left his kayak on a rack, with its bow pointed toward his house, signifying that the craft had brought home seal. The wife carried the meat inside.

The head, complete with eyes, nose, mouth, and whiskers but with the skull removed, was hung on the wall facing the entrance. The hunter then went to the men's house to change

A NUNIVAK HUNTER. *Christian name: Thomas Toots, grandfather of Alice Smith. Ivory labrets.* E. S. Curtis, Special Collections Division, University of Washington Libraries, Negative No. NA 1996.

clothing. His wife, wearing a waterproof parka, placed a strip of oil blubber in a lamp and lit it. This, with the seal's bladder and a bowl of food, she brought to her husband. She distributed seal oil and meat to the old people present, then departed.

While the people around him sang his childbirth song, the hunter inflated the bladder and attached it to a sooted stick. He hung it in his place in the men's house, where it would be kept until the Bladder Feast. In the morning the meat was stored away and the kayak's nose again pointed seaward so that its spirit could watch for game.

➤

One of the many charitable "giveaway" ceremonies of the Nunivak was the Summer Hunting Ceremony, held during July. An experienced hunter called out to the villagers to prepare, and all began to gather together excess gear, weapons, clothing, oil, and food.

The entire village assembled in the men's house. The oldest man's daughter danced while everyone sang. Then the oldest man brought in their gifts, all of which were generously divided among the helpless, the elderly, the crippled, and the widowed. In this way, the unfortunate gained enough supplies to last through the coming winter. As the gifts were distributed, the people prayed that the spirits would look kindly upon their generosity toward one another and aid them in the summer hunt.

Even children were honored with pomp and ceremony when they achieved something of worth—catching their first bird. The bird was brought to the men's house, where the father covered the bird with a young hair-seal skin. To ward off any evil influence, the boy was clad in a waterproof parka, and he offered the spirit-empowered sealskin to an old man, who in return would skin the bird. During the skinning, those present sang a birth song for the boy. From this time on, the birth song was the boy's possession.

The boy's mother offered berries mixed with grease to the old people, and other relatives offered dried fish. As people accepted the food, they threw portions of it to the floor as offerings. They prayed for longer life, for good hunting, and that the boy would grow up healthy and become a successful hunter. With a firm respect for the infirmities that await the elderly, the villagers also prayed that the boy would always be able to eat his game.

LEGENDS

Monster Serpents and Cannibal Dwarfs

➤

Imagination and a highly developed intuition are Eskimo calling cards. The mythology and tales of the Bering Strait peoples convey a wide range of storytelling skills and are a testament to their moral timber.

Many variations exist in the early tales, depending on the teller and his location. For instance, there are slight variations between the legend Curtis collected at Cape Etolin and that from Nash Harbor regarding the origins of Nunivak Island. Oral history changes slightly with each retelling; just as the seasons change and the weather fluctuates, so do the tales.

At Cape Etolin in 1927, Curtis heard one elder's story of how Nunivak Island was created. Two brothers, one strong and one younger and weaker, were out at sea when a stiff blow came up. For protection, they tied up on the leeward side of some anchor ice. By the second day of the storm, the younger brother began to whimper and cry out. The elder warned, "Do not cry so. Schlumyoa [spirit of the universe, sun, moon, stars, and earth] will hear you."

The boy kept crying. Suddenly they saw a spirit being descending from the sky toward them. The elder said, "At last the spirit has heard you. Do not be afraid now, you who cried."

The spirit stood with one foot on each kayak. She wore a woman's parka of white fish skin, and she carried something inside it. The elder brother explained, "My brother has been crying since yesterday. I told him to hush and not to call down a spirit."

"As soon as I heard, I knew someone needed aid, so I came to you," said the spirit. With these words, she scattered something on each side of the kayak. This became land, while the ice they were tied to turned into a mountain in the middle of the land. She sprinkled something more, which became plants and animals. The younger brother discovered himself changed into a woman. Since then, woman has always been weaker than man. From these two descended the people of Nunivak.

Young people are instructed never to yell loudly while they are in the village, because

Schlumyoa might hear and, thinking it a real call of distress, come to give aid. If Schlumyoa is called needlessly, she may not come when one is in real trouble.

The Nash Harbor version of the origin of Nunivak Island, as told to Curtis in 1927, picks up where the Cape Etolin story leaves off. After the elder brother and the boy-turned-woman are married, the man becomes a great hunter, who is able to provide everything in great plenty.

Once, while he was away hunting, his bowstring broke, so he returned home to have his wife make him a new one. As she was shredding sinew, he lay beside her watching, and he began to playfully tease her. When she edged away, he moved toward her, continually teasing, until at last she thrust her sinew threader toward him. This she did many times, whenever he moved closer. Finally, he became very still. Frightened by his quietness, she looked at him very carefully. His body was full of tiny holes. She carried his corpse outside and buried it in the snow.

That night, the spirit woman entered and inquired after the man. "My husband broke a bowstring and came home for a new one. He went out again and has not returned since," the wife lied.

Not quite satisfied with the answer, the spirit searched the house and asked repeatedly, "Did he really go?"

"Yes," the wife replied. "He went away, taking his new bowstring with him."

One winter night, as the woman built her fire, the smoke hung in the room instead of billowing through the smokehole. She went outside to build a windbreak. While she was busy, the spirit woman returned and sat down in the snow to watch. The spirit felt something protruding into her back, which felt like a human knee bone. She dug, and found the body of the man, punched full of holes.

"Why did you lie to me?" the spirit woman asked.

"He was teasing me, but I only motioned at him with my sinew threader and that happened," replied the wife.

"Why did you do that? You were intended to live together as man and wife," said the spirit.

The woman sprang to her feet to run away. As she did so, the spirit woman reached out to grab her, but the spirit only managed to graze her foot. As the Nunivak woman disappeared, she sang a song: "Up shall I go, up shall I go, to the middle of the sky shall I go. Where all the spirits go, there shall I go. Up shall I go."

The spirit woman was very distressed that the great hunter whom she had helped prosper had been killed and that his wife had gone to the sky. The spirit woman broke her knife in two and inserted the halves into her upper jaws to make long fangs. Then she turned into a wolf, and all of her wolf offspring later became humans who lived on Nunivak Island.

➤

Other tales served to dramatize sudden and inexplicable death. In a village of many people, in such a remote and inherently dangerous land, men disappeared each year. Men would go out caribou hunting and never return. Men would paddle out to sea in kayaks and not be heard from again.

People wondered. One time the son of the greatest hunter of the village set out for caribou. He stopped to cook food by a large rock, and he saw something coming over the horizon, growing larger as it approached.

A monster, with a huge head and body and many legs, trundled past his hiding place. The body was so long it stretched beyond the horizon, and although the legs ran all day, the monster did not pass the young man. At dusk, the legs and body stopped moving, then began to run back in the direction from which it had

come. As the head passed, the youth saw that the monster had taken a caribou and a man from his village.

The monster stopped near the rock and cried, "Someone has been watching me! My body feels someone nearby." Badly frightened, the young man managed to remain quiet until the monster went on its way and disappeared over the horizon. He ran back to the village but told no one what he had seen.

The two following years, the young man saw the monster while he was out on hunting trips, but he hid and remained silent about it in the village. The third year, he prepared his hunting gear and set out in his kayak.

After five days of paddling he came to a steep rock jetty jutting far into the sky from the water's edge. On one side of the rock were carved stairs, and he climbed to the top, where the monster made its home. The young man hid near the monster's house and heard the beast tell its wife, "I cannot hunt in a small place like this. I must go a long distance from here."

The monster uncoiled its long body and started off in the direction of the young man's village. All day, the body and legs ran past him.

When they stopped, he chopped at the body with an axe. He threw all his strength to the task but was unable to cut the monster. Under the force of his blows, however, the monster's body bent and sagged until it touched the water. Soon that portion of the body sank and dragged down with it the rest, until finally the monster's head sank, and it drowned.

The young man searched the monster's rock and discovered two caches, one filled with caribou carcasses and the other filled with human bodies. He heard voices as he conducted his search, so he hid. Two people approached in a kayak. When they reached the top of the rock, one said, "I'll take the caribou. You take the humans."

The other answered, "No, you always take the humans." Then the two went into the hut. Later, the young man crawled up on the roof and peeped through the smokehole. He saw two women and their parents, sleeping. He entered and cut off their heads, but the heads awoke and bounded up and down, jumping over to their eating bowls, where they ate as though nothing had happened. The young man clubbed the heads, which snapped and bit at him, until at last they were dead.

He paddled back to his village, where he told his people what had happened. "Now the men can hunt caribou without being in danger."

➤

Perhaps the most outlandish and yet revealing of the Nunivak tales concerns the Cannibal Dwarfs. Dwarfism, syphilis, and many other disfigurements and diseases were known to exist in the prehistory of Alaska's first peoples, prior to Russian contact.

This story also feeds on the islanders' great fear that one of their own would venture too far afield from home, be taken in, and then tricked or murdered by a rival tribe.

A young woman and her brother lived so far inland that they had no knowledge of the sea.

While still young, the boy provided for both by fishing, snaring mink, and netting squirrels, and his sister would accompany him. But when he became a man, his sister remained at home. He became a great hunter, and his caches were always filled with squirrel and caribou skins.

One late afternoon, when in need of meat, the young man set off for caribou, against his sister's objections because of the lateness of the hour. Not far from home, he came upon a caribou herd and shot one, which limped away wounded. He gave chase, but it was long after dark before he killed and skinned the animal.

Unable to find the trail home in the dark, he wrapped himself in the fresh skin and slept. All winter he wandered through that country, unable to find his way home. Summer came, and by that time he had reached the ocean, which was so vast he was unable to see the opposite shore. His boots were worn through, and his parka was tattered. One day, exhausted, he fell beside a stack of freshly piled driftwood. Not long afterward, he heard dogs howling, and soon two men, who were brothers, came by. Seeing his emaciated condition, they carried him to the men's house in their village.

While he was recuperating, his rescuers told him, "You are just breathing [your life is in danger]. Some day some people here will cause you trouble."

Just then the brothers heard shouting outside and knew that a visitor was approaching the village. The young man saw that the stranger was his sister with her dog. She said to him, "The dog smelled your tracks and trailed you here."

Later, while sitting in the men's house, the young man was approached by a boy messenger, who said, "You, the stranger, must come with me."

DAHCHIHTOK, NUNIVAK ISLAND. *Christian name: Margaret Roger.* E. S. Curtis, Special Collections Division, University of Washington Libraries, Negative No. NA 2002.

"Who wants him?" asked the brothers.

"My sister wants him," said the youth.

The brothers tried to warn the young man not to go with the messenger, telling him he might not return alive.

But he followed the messenger to the home of his sister, who was crying. The young man tried to comfort her and she sobbed when he finally rose to leave. "When will I see you again?" she cried.

The young man saw her parents in the room, two dwarfs (*jusuhhat*, "little people"), who said to him, "We pity you when you leave."

When they began to prepare food for him, their promising future son-in-law, the girl said to him, "Do not eat their food. Come and sit with me on this bench."

The dwarfs offered him human fat in a bowl. In place of it, he ate a bowl of caribou meat that the girl handed him. After going to bed that night with his new wife, she said, "I wonder how long you and I will be able to live together."

He could not fall asleep, worried about what the dwarfs might do to him. As he dozed off toward morning, he was awakened by a crackling sound and the sting of smoke in his nostrils. The house was ablaze. He dashed through the entrance, his clothing and skin scorched. Outside, his wife was crying because she thought he had been burned to death. But the wicked dwarfs were dancing and laughing. They admonished their daughter for crying; they had hoped their son-in-law was about to become their next meal.

The young man, enraged, threw the dwarfs into the fire. His wife told him, "You cannot kill them, no matter how hard you try. They will be back soon."

He went alone to the men's house, where his rescuers and his sister were glad to see him alive and whole. The following day, the messenger entered and again asked the young man to go back and help his sister escape the dwarfs. Against his friends' and sister's wishes, he went back to the dwarfs' home and found his wife there, her eyes swollen from crying.

The dwarfs again prepared food for him, but he ate caribou meat instead when he saw that the dish contained a human hand.

At midnight he awoke just as the house, set in flames again, had collapsed. He was overcome. He came to consciousness in a strange men's house, and all about him were dwarfs, sharpening skin knives. He noticed his own dog beside him. "Our niece has brought us a relish to go with the man meat!" they exclaimed.

The dog, which was very large and vicious, was an *ahlgalunuh* (polar bear) in dog's form. The man mounted the dog's back, and the two floated up through the smokehole, escaping the clutching hands of the dwarfs.

Hearing his parents-in-law inside calling for his skin, the young man snatched a club and ran into the house, smashing their bodies and throwing the pieces into their men's house. They were never seen again in the village.

He went to the village men's house, where he found his two rescuers, his sister, his wife, and his wife's brother, the messenger. As time went by, he often hunted with his wife's brother, going out with him in the spring to catch seal.

One day, when the two were hunting together, the young man killed a seal and stepped out of the kayak onto an ice floe to skin and cut up the carcass. The messenger paddled off. "Why are you paddling away in my kayak?" the young man asked.

"You killed my father and mother" was the answer, and the messenger started back for the village, leaving his companion on a drifting ice floe. When the young man did not return, his sister and the dog traversed the shore, searching. At each village they inquired after the missing man, and at one stop they were informed that a man on an ice floe had passed by during a heavy storm, but he was too far out for the people to go and get him.

While walking along the shore, the dog suddenly stopped and sniffed the air. He plunged into the water, swimming until he disappeared from view. After a long wait, she saw the dog again, carrying her brother on his back. They journeyed back toward the village. Close to it, they halted, and the young man told the dog, "The people here have played many tricks on us. Now we must do something to them, but my two rescuers and their wives are not to be harmed. You go to the village, select a man for a husband to my sister, and take a wife for yourself. Do as you please with the rest of the people."

When the dog returned to them, his jaws, flanks, and breast were flecked with blood. Entering the village, brother and sister found that all the people had been killed with the exception of those they had instructed the dog to let live. The survivors then struck camp and went to live inland at the original homesite of the young man and his sister.

King Island

The Foretelling of Christ the King

➤

Ninety miles northwest of Nome and fifty miles southward from Cape Prince of Wales, King Island's sheer cliffs rise 700 feet above sea level. This two-square-mile island was named Ooq-vok, "a place for winter," by the Eskimos. It is in the direct path of walrus and seal migrations. Amid its mossy vegetation, birds flock, breed, and migrate in the millions. During their nesting season, they inhabit the inaccessible rocky crags along the cliffs.

The Eskimo were primarily walrus hunters, and it is the walrus that first brought the people to the inhospitable island and held them here intact for thousands of years.

On the south side of the island is the only landing area, consisting of a rock slide about 200 feet wide. Few ships ever put in here, with the exception of an occasional trading vessel or an even rarer visit from the revenue cutter. There is no protection from the sea, and the water is too deep for easy anchorage.

In 1927 Curtis found twenty-nine houses scattered irregularly on seven terraces, the lowest some eighty feet above sea level. Because of the sheer cliff, the dwellings were built on twenty-foot stilts, with the rear part of the buildings against the cliff or on poles a few feet high.

Horizontal connecting poles served as drying racks. The two-room homes each sported a front room about sixteen feet long, and a storeroom/porch with a tightly fitting wooden or skin cover. The home was lashed down with a roof of walrus hide; about twelve or thirteen skins were needed to build the house and storeroom or entry. The exterior hides were replaced each year. Between the exterior and interior was a foot-thick filling of moss, providing excellent insulation against the cold, damp weather.

Though he found the living arrangements scrupulously clean, Curtis didn't find the King Islanders, who had left after the summer walrus hunt to work as ivory carvers for the whites in Nome that year, as had become their custom in the past few years. In former times, the King Island people spent the late summer paddling to Siberia, Kotzebue, the Diomedes, and Cape Prince of Wales to exchange walrus hides, meat, and oil for the skins of beaver, fox, and deer, and for berries and fish. As they journeyed along the coast, they gathered driftwood for their own use

and for trade. About September, the people would gather in boats near Port Clarence, trading with the Sledge Island and Teller people for deer and moose. When all had gathered, they paddled home to King Island on a good day and sang songs all the way home.

When Curtis came, only the people's dogs had been left on the island for the summer in great numbers, subsisting on whatever they could hunt or on walrus carcasses left behind for that purpose. Curtis caught up with the islanders later in Nome and interviewed many for his text material.

The photographer called King Island "one of the most picturesque spots in all the North," yet he found it curious that there wasn't even the slightest anchorage protection from storms. "Truly humans pick strange places in which to exist," he mused in his field diary.

Paul Tiulana is one of the traditional chiefs of the King Island people. He was born on King

THE BOW DRILL, KING ISLAND. E. S. Curtis, Special Collections Division, University of Washington Libraries, Negative No. NA 2021. _____

Island in the early 1920s before any white man came to live there and was named Tiulana after his grandfather. His Christian name, Paul, came later when he was baptized by a priest who brought "Christ the King" to the island, a statue of Jesus the Eskimos labored with ropes to place atop the island. It is said that the shining statue can be seen from Little Diomede on a good day.

In 1987 Tiulana and Vivian Senungetuk wrote the book *A Place for Winter,* about Tiulana's years on King Island. Tiulana explains the seasons in detailed Eskimo terms, the coming of white men, and how "Christ the King" chased away a demon who lived on the other side of the island.

The statue was immediately accepted by the islanders because ten years beforehand, an elder had dreamed about it. He said a really shiny thing had come down from the sky and landed where "Christ the King" came to stand.

Another elder had told Tiulana when he was a small child about a medicine man long ago

NOATAK MAN. E. S. Curtis, Special Collections Division, University of Washington, Negative No. NA 2047.

who said that the universe had a creator. "He said if you eat the flesh and drink the blood of this universe's creator, you will be safe. This was before anyone on King Island had heard anything about Christianity."

Most revealing are Tiulana's glimpses into the delicate web of family relationships that existed among the traditional people, subtleties Curtis and his assistant did not pick up on during their brief summer in the Arctic.

Tiulana tells how he always had to give away his first polar bear, his first bird, his first seal to an older person, one who did not hunt much anymore. In this way, the older people would teach him what he needed to learn about the ice, weaponry, and the animals he hunted.

"Our behavior was controlled by relationships. When a person was bad, when a person started to make problems for another person, relationships came in," Tiulana wrote.

Cross-cousins and partner cousins were extremely important in King Island culture and offered a counterbalance in village government. Cross-cousins were supposed to tease one another, make fun when somebody did something wrong. Partner cousins were supposed to help one another throughout life.

Cross-cousins were told when their counterparts did something wrong, and they would make up jokes or songs about the "bad apple" to make him feel funny inside. Partner cousins worked together closely, and one would feel bad for the other if he or she was in trouble.

"Sometimes things happened," Tiulana wrote. "A person had a big mouth and made things hard for another person, over and over. Finally the trouble-maker would be killed. Nobody would care. People would say, 'He asked for it.' When a murder happened, the uncle of the murdered person, or some other relative, could decide to take revenge, maybe kill the murderer. He could do this to satisfy himself but this upset the village further. If the person who was killed was really bad anyway, the people would say, 'He asked for it.' There would be no really hard feelings in the village.

"Mostly we used our dancing to try to take out our frustrations that we had among ourselves. If we did not have anything to do, because the weather was bad, we got frustrated. Dancing, singing, and laughing with each other cured the frustrations of our people."

Tiulana seemed homesick for King Island when I last saw him perform with the King Island Dancers at the Anchorage Museum of History and Art in the summer of 1992. He and his people had been forced from their island home in the late 1960s, when the Bureau of Indian Affairs closed the school and relocated the islanders to Nome and Anchorage.

Tiulana lives in Anchorage now. He and the King Island Dancers perform widely, and he does everything he can to help his people adjust to the complexities of urban life. According to Tiulana, BIA told his people in 1969 that a rock atop King Island would fall down on them and crush their village if they didn't move away. "I was back to King Island just last summer," said Tiulana. "And you know, that rock is still up there."

LEGENDS

Tall Tales of Land and Sea

➤

King Island, according to ancient legend, was once a fish. A man who lived on the mainland once speared a large bullhead in a river. The fish thrashed about so violently that a salt lake was formed. The fish towed the man's kayak swiftly down a stream to the ocean. The man thrust another spear into its side. The pain-crazed fish flung itself into a frenzy, forming what is now called Grantley Harbor. Before the man was able to make his kill, the fish had towed him out of sight of land. When the line slackened, he began to tow the monster toward home, paddling hard.

Tired out, he finally looked back to see what progress he had made. Astonished, he found that he hadn't even traveled the length of his kayak. The magnificent fish had turned into King Island; the hole where the line was attached can still be seen. Frightened, the man cut the line and paddled home at full speed.

The man said nothing about what had happened to him. One day he invited a youth from a poor family to go hunting with him. He told the young man the story, and the pair set out to see if the fish had truly become an island.

They paddled far across the open water, and finally before them rose the rocky banks of the island. On shore, the youth chased birds for so long that the man, chafing impatiently, set out for home alone. Finding himself marooned, the young man made a home in a cave. He survived the winter by eating dead seal and whale that washed ashore.

The following summer, the man, curious as to the fate of the youth, paddled to the island. Seeing the kayak approach, the young man hid and did not answer when his searcher called for him. The man thought that the youth must have starved, so he hiked up the cliff to see if he could locate the body. The youth jumped into his kayak and paddled away. "You deserted me on this island! Now you can stay and live as I lived; but I am leaving a supply of food, although you left me nothing." The man died that winter of starvation. When the young man returned the following summer, he did not find the body.

➤

Another story concerns the first woman who came to King Island after it had been fashioned from a fish. No one knows where she came

59

from or how she came ashore. She built a hut of grass and cut up much meat for a winter cache. After some time she noticed that the carcasses, as she cut them, came to life and bled from their noses. Then, morning after morning, on waking she discovered that part of her parka hood was gone. She knew someone had been with her. One night she awoke to find a man standing inside her hut.

"You have been coming here all fall and winter," she said to the man. "I did not see you or know who you were."

The man told her he had felt sorry for her because she was alone. He told her, "You and I are married. Now I must hurry. It is light and I may be too late to see someone."

The man always returned with much meat. The woman came to understand that her husband was Polar Bear. Someone else was hunting game for her, too, and left her many seals, but neither she nor her husband could discover who it was. One night, Black Whale in human form entered the hut, very angry because Polar Bear had married the woman. His gifts of seal had been his courtship. The two fought inside the house. Polar Bear cried, "There is not room to fight here. Let us go outside."

They struggled on the beach in their own forms—Polar Bear with snarling teeth and slashing claws, Black Whale lashing out viciously with his giant tail. Finally, Bear lodged himself on top of Whale's back and sunk his teeth into Whale's nose. "I can fight no longer, I am giving up," Whale cried, and dove back into the sea.

Polar Bear transformed himself once again into human form. He lived peacefully with his wife from then on.

➤

The legend of the gleaming belt ornament is fanciful and more playful than many of the traditional Eskimo tales. Yet, for all its whimsy, this very old King Island story has its share of gruesome details.

A fine young hunter lived with his parents in a house built on a flat rock. His old mother, worn and tired from hard work, said to him, "I am tired. I need a daughter-in-law to help me. You must marry."

The young hunter went out hunting birds on the top of the island. He came to a rock-bound pool, where five girls were swimming. He stole their clothes and teasingly refused to return them. To four of the girls he then threw the clothes, garment by garment. When dressed, they emerged from the water and flew away as geese.

The fifth girl, too shy to speak, hung her head, not even pleading for her garments back. He returned everything but her belt ornament. She was sad without it, because she was therefore unable to fly like her sisters. He led her to his home. She found the odors there so strong she had to hold her nose. She could eat no oil or meat, so the young man gathered grass seeds and roots for her from the pond.

Learning of this girl who had come from who knows where, the headman, who had two wives, desired her for himself. When the girl refused to go to the headman, he sent a messenger to demand four ducks of the young hunter. The hunter complied, throwing the ducks inside the headman's house. Another messenger was sent, this time demanding four cranes. These the young man soon obtained from the pond. The headman, angry that the hunter was able to fulfill his demands, next asked for something that could talk.

The wife now spoke to her perplexed husband. "Somewhere in the world is something that can talk, but I do not know where it is. When you seek it, you must take nothing but my belt ornament. Your father will give you a

AT NOATAK VILLAGE. E. S. Curtis, Special Collections Division, University of Washington, Negative No. NA 2045.

staff that will show you the way. I shall make extra boots. I can not go home anymore, and the headman of our village will take me while you are away."

The man set out. Wherever he raised his staff and let it go, it fell in the direction he was to follow. When he had gone so far that both his pairs of boots were worn out, he came to a mountain so steep that its slopes could not be scaled. He called out for help. One of his wife's sisters suddenly appeared and flew him to the mountaintop. She gave him food and new boots and sent him on his way. Two other sisters aided him, and the fourth, hearing his story, asked, "What have you got to give in exchange for this thing that talks?"

"I have only the belt ornament of my wife, your sister," he answered.

"If your power is strong, you will soon arrive at a place where the headman lives alone in the men's house. Two men armed with knives guard the door. They kill all strangers who try to enter.

Show the ornament to them, and they will be blinded by its gleam. In the entranceway are six more guards, but dazzle their eyes and pass by. Inside lives the headman, who possesses the thing that talks."

The man wore his boots out walking so far, but he finally came upon the headman's house. He showed the two guards the belt ornament. They were so dazzled they let him pass. Once inside, the six men with knives stopped him, but he blinded them too with the ornament and slipped inside the door of the men's house.

Two more men stopped him. "How did you enter?" they asked. "That person there, our headman, who is in two pieces, will kill us for letting you enter."

"The guards asked me to enter and speak to your headman," replied the young man.

The headman who was cut in two pieces sat up, scolded the guards for allowing a stranger to enter, bade the man to sit beside him, and said, "No one, no matter how wealthy, can see me. How did you, with no gifts and no wealth, pass by my men?"

The young man brought out the belt ornament and dazzled the headman's eyes. He gazed at it covetously. "If you will give it to me," the headman said, "I shall give you anything you desire. I shall have a house built for you such as this."

The young man refused. The headman offered him half of all he owned. The young man said no. The headman offered him his cook, who brought food to them and set it

KING ISLAND HOUSES, 1927. E. S. Curtis, PCA 49-11, Alaska State Library.

before them with unseen hands. Again the young man said, "It is not enough."

"I shall show you my guard," said the headman, lifting a box from a shelf that contained an ivory figure on a chain, armed with a knife. The headman commanded it, "Come out of the box, but do not harm us."

The figure jumped out of the box and walked about the room, his knife held ready to strike. The man refused to take it. The headman asked, "I have offered you everything. What more do you want?"

"Let me try these things."

At the headman's order, the unseen cook brought food and the guard walked about ready for the young man's command to strike. It spoke to the man: "You have bought me and I am yours." The young man accepted, saying to his host, "I have at last found the thing that talks. Let us trade."

While preparing to leave with his new possessions, he was given a boat by the headman, who said, "Take my kayak. It will carry you anywhere you want to go, but be sure to send it back."

The staff directed his way, the unseen cook served him food, and the boat bore him home to King Island. But when he arrived home, he found that his wife had been taken by the resident headman. He strode to the men's house. When the headman saw him enter, he asked, "Did you bring for me the thing that talks? Let me hear his voice and I shall return your wife."

Hiding his anger, the young man directed his invisible cook to serve a meal. Then he brought forward the box with the carved figure. To the headman he said, "Here is the thing that talks. It will speak to you in its own way."

He opened the box, and to the figure he commanded, "If you do not like this headman, kill him, but leave the people unharmed."

The headman tried to pick up the ivory figure but it stabbed his hand. Then it thrust its knife through the headman's heart. The man took his wife home, and took along the headman's wives to be his servants.

➤

Other tales, such as a story about a man who wished to become a medicine man, were intended as moral lessons. In the case of the would-be medicine man, the lesson was "Don't seek what you are not prepared to find."

This man wished to become a medicine man so that his fame would spread and many children would be named for him. He went to visit his cousin, who was a medicine man, and they talked long into the night. He asked his cousin to help him. His cousin only laughed.

The village became quiet and all were asleep. The man rose to go home. Fearfully, he said, "It is long after dark and I had better go home, but perhaps a spirit might get me on the way."

His cousin derided him. "How can you expect to become a medicine man if you are afraid of spirits?"

The man was embarrassed by his own fear, yet he once more asked his cousin to accompany him home. The medicine man refused, saying, "I can see you as you go, dark as it is. I shall be watching over you."

The man began his long walk home. Approaching the village, he was frightened to see something standing near the men's house. Looking at the person's feet, he saw that they hovered a short distance above the ground, the sign of a spirit.

He ran. The spirit followed. He stopped. The spirit stopped. He stood still a long time, trying to slow the rapid beating of his heart. Finally he thought to himself, "If I stand here all night, I shall not live, no matter how strong I am."

DRILLING IVORY, KING ISLAND. E. S. Curtis, Special Collections Division, University of Washington Libraries, Negative No. NA 2020.

He ran downhill toward the men's house, followed closely by the spirit. He vaulted the whalebone fence around the smokehole, thinking to drop through it and escape, but the cover was fastened tight. He lay still on the smokehole, hidden in smoke and steam, watching as the spirit walked about the roof. He heard it say, "If a man truly falls through this hole, I cannot get him."

Hearing this, the man jumped up and ran to the entrance, throwing himself inside to safety.

Looking out, he saw the spirit standing in the hallway. Rising up because of all the commotion, an old man awakened and asked what was happening. "What has this thing been trying to do to me all night? I am very tired from running. Please chase it away!"

The old man threw many things, but the spirit stood its ground. Finally, the old man rubbed together a stone knife and a stone lamp cleaner. These he threw at the spirit, which at once disappeared, for these things drive away spirits.

The man never again tried to become a medicine man.

Diomede Islands

TRADITIONAL LIFE

Where Women Honored Whales

➤

During the Cold War between the United States and the U.S.S.R., Soviet lookouts on Big Diomede Island could stare through binoculars across the water and wave at their American counterparts on Little Diomede Island.

The Diomedes are in the center of the Bering Strait, between the Alaska mainland at Cape Prince of Wales and the Russian outpost of East Cape, Siberia. Through the middle of the narrow strait that separates the two islands passes the international boundary line between the United States and what was once the Soviet Union.

Terrible storms sweep down out of the Arctic and hurl their force toward the Diomedes. Thick fog often enshrouds the islands, and the wind-driven ice floes pile against its granite cliffs. In the brief summer months, the Diomedes stand in the path of several whale migrations, and the walrus and seal herds rest here on their northward and southward treks. Birds flock, breed, and migrate each year to these islands in countless numbers.

Little Diomede rises from the sea, its sheer cliffs supporting low-growing mosses and berries. In Curtis's day, the island people lived in an aggregation of stone houses on terraces, on a slope just above a gravel spit that in ancient times served as a walrus haul-out.

The exterior walls of the family houses were stacked with boulders, framed inside with four large uprights at each corner, connected with beams at the eaves. Whale jawbones arched to form solid roof supports, and shorter beams extended from the jaws to the eaves as secondary supports. The family homes were roomy, about fourteen feet square and eight and a half feet high. The roof extended slightly beyond the walls and consisted of adzed flat timbers heavily overlaid with earth and sod. Interior walls and the floor were crafted from wooden splits. Light and ventilation came through the smokehole covered with seal or walrus intestine parchment. A wide bench ran around the room, and above the bench were racks attached to the eaves for hanging clothing and weapons. Stone oil lamps were used for heating and cooking.

A hole in the floor provided a tunneled entranceway, with a passage about twenty feet long, four feet high, and about three feet wide, gradually widening to ten feet at the outside entrance. This space, lined with stones, provided an excellent dry storage area for small boats, nets, and utensils. On the roof of the entranceway was a small wooden storehouse, covered with walrus hide tightly lashed down and used to stow away dried food, clothing, and furs. Caches used to store oil pokes, meats, and berries were dug near the houses and sealed with wooden covers weighed down with stones.

The men's house, the *kuzugi,* was constructed similarly, except on a larger scale. Curtis noted that the men's house was not as complete or extensive as the men's house on Nunivak and attributed this to the fact that the Diomedes' family homes were more spacious and their ceremonies were more family oriented in nature. Curtis did not find ceremonies comparable to the Bladder, Messenger, and Asking Feasts here, which involved the entire village. The Diomede people celebrated whale and seal hunting com-

MEN AND DOGS IN UMIAK, STARTING UP THE NOATAK RIVER, KOTZEBUE. E. S. CURTIS, PCA 49-3, ALASKA STATE LIBRARY.

munally with distribution, feasting, and dancing in the fall. Similar festivities were also held in the spring. Family ceremonies heralded the naming of children and the first bird or animal catch by a youth.

Hides, meat, and oil not used for subsistence were traded by the Diomede people on both sides of the Bering Strait in exchange for land animal furs, river fish, and other products.

In contrast to other places Curtis visited, the Diomedes included a woman as an important part of their whaling ritual. When the whaling season was upon them, the steersman, harpooner, and two members of a whaling crew, all wearing mittens and parkas and carrying ice scrapers and staffs, would walk to the southern end of the island to pick a willowy shrub of the species used to tie the mouths of their oil pokes. They brought this back to the village with them, and carried all their boat gear, lines, pokes, paddles, and weapons into the steersman's house. Once inside, they barred the entrance with a stick. The crew prepared the equipment, aided in the sewing, when necessary, by a chosen woman. Within the house, other than the boat crew, were only an old man, who had been chosen to conduct the ceremony, and a woman who symbolized the whale spirit and was considered a member of the crew.

When all was in order, the old man sat on the bench by the rear wall, with steersman and harpooner on each side of him. The woman sat in the middle of the floor, and the two crew members sat on opposite walls. The old man sang and drummed the ceremonial songs, songs that had descended from father to son and belonged to and could only be used by the crew. After the singing was done, all the gear was carried outside, and the crew, aided by the villagers, took the boat from its rack and placed each article of the hunt in its proper place. To ward off evil, the crew all donned new clothing and pulled on waterproof parkas and mittens. In procession, led by the old man with the woman in the rear, the group proceeded to the roof of the house. The woman carried a water bucket and a dish of reindeer fat, a portion of which was molded into the form of a whale to signify that the boat was going on a whale hunt. The party circled the roof once clockwise, then returned to the boat, in which the woman placed her bucket and her dish.

The crew now unloaded the boat and turned it bottom side up, the upper gunwale supported by two short poles and the harpoon placed in the bow. While a fire was passed beneath the craft, the woman dipped a small grass mat in urine and carefully washed the harpoon, singing a ceremonial song as she worked. When the song ended, the harpooner shoveled the fire onto a walrus shoulder blade, carried it to the shore ice, and dumped it there.

Again the boat was reloaded. Four inflated pokes were tied in pairs to the craft, with one underneath near the bow and another near the stern to prevent injury to the boat when it was dragged to the water.

As the crew took their positions in the boat, the woman faced them with her water bucket and dish. The crew howled like wolves four times and raised their paddles in the air, while the woman danced and sang a ceremonial song over the whale molded in fat. At its finish, the crew stood clear of the boat while the old man picked up the steering paddle and walked around the craft, tapping it on each side of the bow so that the whale might hear and approach this boat. Singing, he grasped the stern and raised it four times.

Howling, the crew then seized the boat and rushed it to the shore, passing to the left of the woman. Then they returned to her with the boat. She placed her dish of fat in the boat and grasped hold of a short length of walrus intestine, filled with bone ashes. These she scattered as she walked toward the shoreline at the command of the old man behind her, followed by the boat crew with their boat and all the children of the village. The woman and entourage halted at the very edge of the shore, and while she stood with her offering, the old man with the steering paddle sang. When the song ended, the woman cut up the fat into strips and distributed it to the children, who scampered home.

The crew ceremoniously launched the boat, taking their places, and gave four strong paddle strokes before they stopped. The woman sang. When her song was ended, she turned her back to the crew, and they paddled toward her. The harpooner made as if to drive his weapon into her, since the woman now represented the whale and the motion a successful cast. The harpooner now laid down his weapon, and the crew pulled their craft up on shore, took out all the equipment, and turned the boat over it.

They returned home, with the old man in the lead, and all the other villagers were invited to enter for a feast that lasted until nightfall, when the smokehole was covered and a medicine man was called in to ensure that everything had been carried out properly. Once the medicine man had given his approval, the smokehole was uncovered and many stories told.

The following morning, if conditions were good, the crew would depart to hunt whales. To ensure the crew's safety, it was customary for the old man and the woman who took part in the ceremony to remain in the house until the boat returned.

When a whale was distributed, the owner or steersman of the boat received the right half of the head to the fluke. The other half of the head was divided, and the body to the left fluke was distributed to the crew. The crew also received twenty pieces of whalebone. The woman from the ceremony took her share from among smaller portions of the whale's body. The harpooner, additionally, took a right front flipper, a section from the largest bone as long as a man's leg from foot to knee, and a section from the smallest bone the length of the foot of the largest man in the village. A boat that had been employed as a secondary harpoon received that portion from the head to the left flipper. The remainder of the whale was divided equally among all boats that aided in the hunt.

When the fall whaling season was over, weapons and equipment were quickly overhauled in preparation for walrus hunting. Larger skin boats, with crews of seven or eight men, hunted walrus in open water or along the ice's edge. The crews attempted to cut walrus from the herd and then harpoon them, or to go after single animals. It was considered extremely dangerous for a boat to run with the herd, since in numbers the walrus might attack the boat.

Once the harpoon was cast and the walrus sounded, the crew pelted it with stones each time it surfaced to exhaust the animal. When its fight was gone, the harpoon line was pulled in and the animal was killed.

If only a few walrus were killed, the boat owner or steersman took hide and blubber and meat from the hindquarters of the last three ribs, minus flippers and bones. The harpooner was entitled to the head and the body as far as the fourth rib, with the remainder divided among the crew. When the kill was great, meat, hides, and bones were shared equally.

Sea lions were also speared from a boat or harpooned through the ice, and seals were killed by the same method or harpooned on open water from smaller boats.

Before trade brought the use of firearms into play, polar bears were hunted with throwing spears. One story concerns a Little Diomede man who surprised a polar bear while out hunting on the ice. The great bear rushed him and

DIOMEDE GIRL. E. S. Curtis, Special Collections Division, University of Washington Libraries, Negative No. NA 2028.

the man cast his spear, but it only grazed the animal's cheek. Enraged, the huge bear picked up the man and hurled him to the ice unconscious. Then the bear pawed the man and flung his broken body into the air several times before lumbering off.

Other hunters, who had watched in horror but had been afraid to attempt a rescue, then rushed to the man, but his body had been crushed. The men gathered courage and gave pursuit to the bear. Once in close range, a hunter threw his spear, but it glanced off the bear's back. The bear rose up and turned, angrily baring his

fangs and snarling. A second hunter seized the opportunity and drove a spear through its belly. A third hunter also scored a hit. The bear fell badly wounded and was dead by the time the other hunters caught up. The man who had made the first hit took the best of the meat and divided the remainder equally among the others.

Another account of a polar bear hunt on the ice near the Diomedes is reflective of the waste-not, want-not traditions that existed then. No hunter took more game than he could carry home. This story also provides insight into the ways in which polar bears hunt together.

"I was hunting on the ice near Big Diomede when I saw three polar bears by the water," one informant recounted. "I crept close and watched them from behind an ice hummock. One bear left and went to an ice hummock, where it kept watch cautiously. This bear was the sentinel. The other two stretched their bodies out flat, close to the water's edge.

"Soon I saw a seal come up. It thrust its head high up and looked around, then dived. Several times I saw the seal's head, and it gradually came closer to the ice. Then, when the seal dived again, one of the bears slipped noiselessly into the sea. Soon the seal broke water, and when it began to splash and thrash about, I knew the bear had attacked it from below. The seal died quickly, and the bear, holding the carcass in its jaws, swam back to the ice. While the bear clung to the ice with one paw, the second bear leaned over the edge, reached out a paw, and with teeth and claws hauled up the seal. The two bears covered the carcass with snow to cool it, while the third kept watch from the hummock. When the seal had cooled, they pushed aside the snow and began to eat."

The sentinel bear then came down from its hummock and took its place at the feast. "As I was getting ready to shoot from behind my hummock, where I had built a little snow wall and thrust my rifle through, I heard shots in the distance. The bears stood up and looked around. Two were frightened and shambled off. I shot the one that was still eating; my bullets went through its hip and chest. The other two were still within easy range, but I did not fire. I could not carry so much meat. I took only the forequarters of my kill and started home. I thought to take a piece of the seal to prove my story, but I did not. On my way, I met two hunters and told them about my good luck. They set out for the meat I had left behind, and I went home."

A Pact of Survival Between Young and Old

➤

When a child was born on Little Diomede, a small fire was lit in the parents' home, and the baby was bathed lovingly in a wooden dish. After its bath, the baby was kept rolled up in a parka until the navel healed. Often with male children, a successful hunter in the village, usually related by blood, would give the baby this birth parka. With this gift of warmth, the hunter signified that he would train the boy to hunt by his own methods. In return, the boy's first catch of each species of game would usually be given to his mentor, or to another village elder.

Life was precious among the Diomede people, and it was common practice to give the child the name of the most recently deceased relative, in order that the name would remain with the family and not be forgotten. Sometimes the child was named for the person most recently deceased in the village. If a person had no relatives and was alone in the world, he might come to the family and ask them to name the baby for him, so that his name would survive after his death.

Once the male baby's navel was healed, he was carried to the beach by his father, where he was given a walrus jawbone to grasp in his tiny fingers. The belief was that if the male child played with the jawbone, he would become a good hunter. The father then returned home, where the mother waited by the entrance, and he gave her the child.

Girls were reared and instructed by their mothers. During their childhood, when they caught their first tomcod or picked their first berries or greens, they were given a feast.

While boys were still young, their fathers presented them with slings with which to cast stones, or with bolas, which spread in flight and covered perhaps three feet of space when fully extended. The boys practiced with them until they were experts. When one of the bola stones touched a bird, the bird's flight changed course and the weapon wrapped around its prey, sending it plummeting to the ground. The boy's first bird was skinned and dried by his father, and a special feast was held in the boy's honor. During

the feast, the parents presented gifts to their friends and relatives, especially cousins, and to any others in the village who might ask for a gift.

Indeed, boys were honored with feasts for each first kill of a species. The animals were given to the man who had presented his parka to the boy at birth. Yet the feasts themselves varied from family to family and were individualized rituals passed down from generation to generation.

As a mark of honor, a boy's head was shaved when he had killed his first polar bear. The slaying of the first sea lion was an occasion for a great feast and the presentation of many gifts. At this time, the youth's head was shaved—even his eyebrows.

In order to gain eligibility for marriage, young men had to first prove that they were adequate providers by killing four of the larger sea mammals, such as sea lions and seals. Either his parents would choose a suitable young woman, or he would woo and win his bride-to-be. In either case, his mother would ask the consent of the girl's parents.

The young man or his parents would prepare and present to the young woman a complete outfit of clothing. The marriage was consummated with the man going to dwell in his new in-laws' home. As a married man, his responsibilities grew. He was now obliged to share his game with both his own and his wife's parents.

If a woman was widowed and chose not to remarry, she often would exchange work for help from villagers. Her own and her deceased husband's parents also provided aid, particularly when there were children.

As in other Eskimo villages, divorce was a simple affair, with the husband returning to his parents' home. Adultery by either partner often resulted in divorce and sometimes in the death of the adulterer.

Death on Little Diomede was highly ritualized. As soon as a person died, the body was dressed in his or her best finery, and deerskin socks were placed on the feet instead of boots. The corpse was straightened, the hands drawn down to the waist and held in place by a belt. If the death took place in the daylight, the body was taken out of the house at once. If the death occurred at night, the body was kept in the house and watched by relatives, who used the body as a pillow to sleep on.

In daylight, the body was lashed to a board and pulled feetfirst through the smokehole in the roof. The feet were pointed to the south in fall or winter, or to the north along the migratory routes in spring or summer. Some of the mourners carried the personal belongings of the deceased on grave boards, while close relatives bore the body by nine lines—four on each side and one, a spear line, in the front. Feetfirst, the body was carried to the top of the mountainside, where stones were rolled to form an ellipse. The body was then placed inside the grave, where it was stripped of its clothes, and the clothing and personal belongings were put into rocky crevices. The grave boards were placed beneath the corpse and on all sides, then the makeshift grave was weighted down with stones.

All the villagers would leave except for the closest relatives, who circled the grave once clockwise, then descended to enter the village from the north, unless it was autumn, when they entered from the south.

One of the relatives carried a stone into the house upon their return. The room was then cleaned throughout and washed down, after which the relatives bathed. The stone was placed in the center of the room, and all stood about and made motions as if to brush the water from their bodies onto the stone, transferring any evil influences to it. This purification rite concluded with the stone being rolled to the beach.

For a man, the period of mourning among relatives lasted four days; for a woman, five days. Yet for ten days after a death, all the relatives would wear their mittens and keep their parka hoods up whenever they left the house. The belief was that if they failed to observe this rite, their hands would become paralyzed or severely weakened.

If the death occurred before or during the crucial fall hunting period, the relatives could do no hunting until game had been brought back to the village by others. If the death took place in spring, the male relatives could not embark in skin boats until meat was brought into the vil-

lage. Violation of these taboos was thought to cause the game animals to avoid the island, thereby resulting in a period of starvation for the entire population.

Spirits of the dead were often believed to wander through the village. If this happened within a year of burial, the spirit wore grave clothes and played harmless pranks. But after a year, spirits who returned had their eyes open and could do great harm. One person's mother had seen a woman who had been long dead sitting by the cooking lamp in her home. "My mother reached out to touch her, but the woman disappeared. The following day, my mother's arm swelled and was very painful for a long time."

Spirits who have outstayed their welcome must be exorcised by medicine men and driven to the land below where the lost and drowned go, called Ub'rik. No spirits could return from Ub'rik, where there was no ocean, and darkness

SELAWIK WOMEN. E. S. CURTIS, SPECIAL COLLECTIONS DIVISION, UNIVERSITY OF WASHINGTON LIBRARIES, NEGATIVE NO. NA 2053.

prevailed. This place was presided over by a long-haired woman.

The spirits of the dead who were properly buried lived in two villages, one at the north end and the other at the south end of the island. The medicine men were the only ones who knew the location of these spirit villages, and they could travel there both in life and after death. In the spirit villages, the dead souls lived in plenty, in the same manner as humans, but it was said that the spirits of the northern village obtained better animals and had better food than the spirits of the southern village.

THE MUSKRAT HUNTER, KOTZEBUE. E. S. CURTIS, SPECIAL COLLECTIONS DIVISION, UNIVERSITY OF WASHINGTON LIBRARIES, NEGATIVE NO. NA 2083.

If the spirits of Ub'rik were thirsty, they would hold back the formation of ice in the fall, which in turn delayed hunting. In this event, a medicine man would be called on to build a fire on the beach, which he let burn down to ash. Then, with his legs in the ashes, he sat on one edge of a waterproof parka and held the other edge with his feet. The sleeves of the parka he held up and shook, so that the spirits below could speak clearly and loudly to the assembled people. They asked their human relatives for fresh water to quench their thirst; this was poured into the outstretched parka of the medicine man. Soon after their thirst was slaked, the fall ice would form and the people could begin the crucial hunt.

In times of famine, it was thought that the spirits from above were taking all the game. The medicine man, with his knowledge of the spirit lands, would be sent up the mountainside to find out whether this was the case. If so, he would order on his return that the people model a seal out of snow. He then took the snow seal to the north and south spirit villages and allowed it to slide down the slope. This act signified that the medicine man had taken the animals from the spirits, and the act would bring plenty of game, particularly seals, to the people.

The medicine man secured his supernatural powers by gaining control of the spirits, both animal and human. But the legends show that spirits often controlled the medicine man, and his failure to understand or carry out their instructions properly could result in his losing his powers and, subsequently, his status.

Spirit powers were handed down from a shaman to his son, a relative, or a close friend, with instructions on how to use them. Spirits would appear to a man when he was alone and far from the village. The man was then artfully instructed in how to use its powers. A man who returned to the village and was able to demonstrate what he had learned eventually assumed the role of shaman.

A spirit also could enter a person's body, making its presence known by emitting weird sounds through the person's mouth. If this happened, villagers would quickly strip the person naked. The spirit would then cause the person to bleed profusely at the mouth and dash about wildly. While still under the spirit's influence, the person was taken to every house in the village, where he pointed out the sick and instructed them as to the causes of their illness.

This type of spirit takeover was thought to give the person supernatural power, but a long time had to elapse before he was allowed to use a drum and be acknowledged as a shaman. During this apprenticeship to the spirits, the would-be shaman had to prove his ability by successful performances.

Headmen on Little Diomede were chosen by the sanction of their fellow villagers. These were rare men with great wisdom, who led by example and by offering learned advice. The qualities sought in a Diomede headman might make an interesting want ad for a U.S. president. "Wanted: One man who shows respect for the aged, including listening to and heeding their advice; gives material aid to the poor and helpless in the form of food and clothing; and possesses natural ability as a hunter and as a leader among men."

LEGENDS

Manina the Medicine Man

➤

The most powerful shaman who ever lived on Little Diomede was a hunter named Manina, whose reputation spread to both Siberia and the Alaskan mainland.

The Little Diomede hunter married a King Island woman. Though not a medicine man in his youth, he, like others on the island, possessed a spirit power. Manina could call this spirit to him by stretching out flat on the floor, with a stick bound to his head. When the spirit entered him, he would fall unconscious, and the villagers would question him on many subjects. If a person could raise Manina's head, the question had been answered in the negative; if the spirit caused Manina's head to become rigid, the answer was affirmative.

Once Manina and his wife, along with several other Diomede people and a medicine man, traveled to King Island to participate in the dances there. The islanders divided into two groups, each trying to outdo the other in dance and song. Manina's group was weaker in song and was losing the contest, so the medicine man drummed and bent his head low to the floor. This was the custom when a shaman was about to send spirits out. He did so this time in order to obtain songs from his spirit powers below.

Suddenly the medicine man called out, "If any man wishes to learn songs from my spirit powers, he must come below with me."

Manina whispered in a low voice to his neighbor that he would like to go below. The medicine man asked, "Who is that man my spirit heard talking and saying that he wished to go below with me? I shall take him, even though he be no medicine man. If he refuses now, my spirit powers will eat him."

Manina's neighbor spoke up, "This is the man."

The medicine man made Manina sit on the floor, with his legs and arms wrapped about the medicine man, who instructed the people that when he laid down his drum, one of them must strike Manina with a grass sock.

When Manina was struck with the sock, he lost consciousness. He awoke in a huge but unfamiliar men's house far below. Amazed, he looked around and discovered that spirits filled the benches all around him. All the spirits in the men's house had once been human. Some of

THE UMIAK, KOTZEBUE. E. S. CURTIS, SPECIAL COLLECTIONS DIVISION, UNIVERSITY OF WASHINGTON, NEGATIVE NO. NA 2042.

them, including the spirit chief Amuktulik, had killed men when they were human beings.

Amuktulik, the spirit chief, sat on a bench along the rear wall. He was terribly ugly, with a sharply slanting mouth on one side of his face. His mumbled words were difficult to discern. The medicine man said, "I have brought Manina here to learn songs."

Amuktulik called for his drum and told Manina he would sing him a song from the mainland. "You must learn it as I sing it," Amuktulik instructed.

Instead of stopping at the end of the song, Amuktulik launched into a series of songs that lasted a long time. When he was finished he handed Manina the drum. "My spirits will eat you if you have not learned my songs," the spirit chief warned.

Even though the spirit chief's words, spewed from his grotesque mouth, had been difficult to comprehend, Manina had learned the songs easily and well. When he finished his recital, all the spirits yelled in delight. Amuktulik was so pleased that he told Manina the spirits would leave the medicine man they had helped so often in the past. "Now we shall be the spirit powers of Manina," Amuktulik declared. "Where are you from?"

"I am not a King Island man," said Manina. "I have come from Little Diomede."

Amuktulik assured him that when he returned to Little Diomede, the spirits would travel with him. "Now go above and repeat these songs," the spirit chief directed.

Once he had returned to the land above, Manina sang so many new songs that his group won the contest. Aided by his new spirit powers, who conjured up a fair wind, Manina and his group quickly returned to Little Diomede.

After his return, Manina became a great medicine man, and his reputation spread far and wide because he could cure the sick, regardless of their ailment.

That winter, Amuktulik commanded Manina to go below the ice so that there would be many seals for his people in the spring. Manina knew that as a medicine man he must do what his spirit power ordered or he would be killed.

The villagers cut a hole in the ice and collected all their ropes, which they tied together and piled inside the men's house in two great stacks. The end of each coil was fastened to the entrance posts. In the evening the men bound Manina, who was clad in a waterproof parka and long mittens, so that his hands were tied behind his back and his ankles were lashed together. While most of the men remained inside the men's house, several of them carried Manina— once he was possessed of his powers—to the hole in the ice, where they plunged him into the cold, black waters. Then the men ran back to the men's house.

Once the ropes ran out to the end and the lines became taut, two men and a woman grasped each rope and hauled it in. As soon as

BERRY PICKERS, KOTZEBUE. E. S. CURTIS, SPECIAL COLLECTIONS DIVISION, UNIVERSITY OF WASHINGTON, NEGATIVE NO. NA 2036.

Manina was dragged through the ice hole, his spirit powers left him. The people worked quickly to strip him of his waterproof parka and mittens. They found seal whiskers in his right mitten, which were ceremoniously distributed among the boat crews. The following spring, a great catch of seal was made by the islanders.

The following winter, Amuktulik upped the ante considerably. The spirit chief instructed Manina to have his head cut off and thrown into the sea. The men cut a hole in the ice and gathered at night in the men's house. Manina ordered that all the lights be extinguished and a single, unlit stone lamp be placed in the middle of the floor. Lying on the floor, Manina instructed his elder brother to use a fire drill on his right eye. The brother twirled the drill rapidly so that the eye of Manina glowed with flame. This flame his brother used to light the stone lamp, and from it all the lamps in the room were lit.

While two men held a waterproof parka under the entrance hole, Manina lay down flat on his back with his head dangling over the entrance. His elder brother grasped a long, sharp knife and cut off Manina's head. As it dropped into the waterproof parka, the two men quickly wrapped the head in the garment and ran to the ice hole, where they cast it into the water. Then the headless body was thrust down through the entrance hole of the men's house, where the spirits ate it. The two men who had taken Manina's head to the ice hole returned, reporting as they came through the entrance that the body had disappeared. The people covered the entrance with a mat and began to sing. At the end of the third song, the elder brother began to sweat and worry. "Why did the people listen to him when he wanted his head cut off?" his brother wailed.

The people continued to sing urgently, and at the end of the fourth song, the mat was lifted. There stood Manina, as well as ever with his head firmly attached to his neck.

Manina's power from then on greatly increased. He could pull from his body anything the people desired. He brought schools of fish, whales, and herds of seal and walrus to Little Diomede.

In the fall, when the ice was coming down from the north, the chief of the spirit powers came again and ordered Manina to kill his own son, Tuktuk, when the ice had solidified.

Day after day, Manina sat in the men's house, grieving and worrying that he would not be able to raise his son from the dead. The ice formed, and still Manina could not bring himself to act on the spirit chief's orders. One day, the wound where Manina's head had been cut off began to bleed freely. He grew so weak that he couldn't speak. When he ordered that preparations be made for the slaying of his son, his voice returned and the neck wound healed.

A long knife and two grass mats from Kotzebue were brought to the men's house. A drummer was chosen, and two men in waterproof parkas screened off one end of the room with a single grass mat. When all the lamps were lit, Manina stood in the entrance hole with a knife in his hand and called for his son.

The people sang many songs, and at the end Manina cried and kissed Tuktuk, then plunged the long blade into his son's neck. The two men caught the body and shoved it behind the grass curtain. Manina then drove the blade into himself and slumped down in the entrance hole. The people covered the entrance hole with the second grass mat.

The people resumed their singing, but below the sound of their low chanting, they could hear the spirits sucking the blood from the two bodies. After all the songs were finished, Tuktuk miraculously rose from behind the curtain and Manina stood up in the entrance hole, their wounds healed. With this resurrection, Manina's fame spread far beyond Little Diomede.

Through these many death-defying trials, Manina developed complete trust in his spirit powers. Finally, Amuktulik came again that summer and instructed Manina to make masks in the fall that resembled all of his spirit powers and one that resembled Manina. "This is the last thing for you to do, and this dance to be held will be all in fun," the spirit chief promised. "Bring the masks and a decorated woman's parka to the men's house. Then cut off your fingers and throw them to the dogs."

All that summer, throughout the long sunlit days and evenings, Manina stayed busy creating the masks. He also made one to represent his first spirit power, before the King Island spirits had come to him and made him such a powerful medicine man. This first spirit, Kangina, was but half a person from head to heels, and the other spirits feared him greatly.

That fall the people gathered, as was their custom, in the men's house, and Manina cut off his fingers and fed them to the dogs. Then he reached his hands out through the entrance hole and when he withdrew them, the people saw that Manina once again had fingers. He covered the entrance hole with the decorated woman's parka, and surrounded it with all his masks.

At once Amuktulik slipped into the parka from below, and hiding his grotesque face behind his raised forearm, he picked up his mask and began to dance while the people sang.

At the end of his song, he dropped the mask and disappeared through the entrance hole. One by one, each spirit power danced. The half-man, half-spirit danced the longest, and the people liked his dancing so much that they called him back several times.

When the dancing ended, Manina stored away his masks in a waterproof parka. Even in the late 1920s, when Curtis visited Little Diomede, the people still held these masked dances. And although shamanism has largely been undermined in the ensuing years by Christianity, even now medicine men, when called by a spirit, must become the spirit itself.

One spring, a party of Siberians, including a powerful medicine man, came to visit Little Diomede. As was the custom, the visitors were invited to sing and dance. After the ceremony, Manina placed a bead in a sling and cast it into the sea. He called, "Bead, return."

The bead returned, but Manina was unable to find it. He asked for a walrus-stomach drumhead, and holding it outright, circled the visitors and his people. Each time he passed by the Siberian medicine man, Manina went very slowly, eyeing the visitor intently. He then ran around the room twice, very fast. He struck the Siberian medicine man with the walrus stomach and ran back a few steps. When Manina shook the stomach, out rolled the bead. It is said that as soon as the Siberian medicine man returned to his homeland, he dropped dead.

Through his supernatural acts, Manina became the greatest medicine man ever to live on Little Diomede. He brought sea mammals near the island in the hunting seasons, cured the sick, and broke up the ice when it filled the straits.

LEGENDS

The Mysterious Whereabouts of Departed Souls

➤

Starvation was an ever-present threat to the Eskimos of the Bering Strait. The tale of Ubuk, from Little Diomede Island, encouraged the people to practice voluntary population control on the island as a way of ensuring a sufficient supply of game. Ubuk's story also serves to illuminate the people's intense symbiotic relationship with the walrus as their sustainer, oceanic teacher, and spiritual equal in the natural world.

Long ago, a gravel bar extended from Little Diomede almost to Big Diomede Island. A couple came to live on Little Diomede. No one knows where they came from. The woman said, "The people will live here forever and never die out." The man replied, "No, if the people live here and multiply fast, they will find it hard to feed a great number."

From this man and woman descended the people of Little Diomede. They subsisted mainly on walrus, which in those days pulled up on each side of the gravel bar to rest. In the fall, the walrus came up from beneath the ice and poked their heads through to breathe. The Eskimos say that even when the ice is thick enough to support a man's weight, the walrus are strong enough to thrust their noses through.

Ubuk, a good hunter, often ran along the ice for sport, slashing walrus on the cheeks with his knife as they came up to breathe. One day he speared a walrus by the edge of the ice pack, and when he tried to let go of the line, he found his hands were stuck fast. He was pulled into the sea and carried far under the cold water. Darting to the surface, the female walrus grabbed Ubuk and rubbed her flippers over his eyes. From then on, he saw as a walrus.

She took off his clothes and they headed south with the herd toward the home of the walrus. When they dove to feed, Ubuk was always the last to reach the bottom, and when they rose to the surface to head ever southward on their journey, he was always behind. They fed on clams, eating them whole, but Ubuk broke his open and ate only the meat inside. Slowly he became starved, thin and weak.

The walrus instructed him to swallow the clams whole so that he would get his fill. "When it is time to go below, look up into the sky and pick a cloud," the walrus told him. "Then kick hard, as if you were trying to touch the cloud, and you will go to the bottom fast."

Ubuk soon regained his strength and was able to keep up with the herd. After a long journey, the walrus came to their home in the south. To Ubuk they seemed to live just as humans did, in houses, with their dead buried behind the village.

He noticed that many of the walrus had scars on their cheeks, and he was told that he had caused their wounds. Sometimes Ubuk craved the food of humans so much that he would steal away behind the walrus village and eat the meat of their dead. The herd objected vehemently to this desecration of bodies, but the chief ordered, "Let him eat. Walrus are the food of humans."

He noticed that the walrus left in bands each summer, some heading to the mainland or to Siberia, others to the Diomede islands, but all returned to their winter village in the south.

Ubuk lived and traveled with the walrus for four years, growing hair on his body and arms like a walrus. Once when his band came up on the shore ice south of his village on Little Diomede, Ubuk stole away and ran home.

The village and his home smelled so strongly that Ubuk found he could not live there, so he set up a walrus-skin tent some distance away, living there until he again became used to the odor of humans. His mother dug many roots for him to eat. After a long time, he was able to return to his home.

Whenever the walrus came by Little Diomede on their migrations south, Ubuk took a boatload of roots out to them. He frequently would dive under the ice and bring his waterproof parka back to the surface brimming with clams for the villagers. When the people needed meat, Ubuk would climb to the top of the mountain and call four times like a walrus. The herd would hear his bark and come to the island.

Ubuk told the people that when he grew old, he would not die on the island but would return to the home of the walrus to the south. One day, Ubuk disappeared, and they all knew he had gone to the walrus.

➤

Another starvation/salvation/strange disappearance story from Diomede drives home a point that no subsistence hunter could afford to ignore: Every animal, large or small, must be treated with the utmost respect and reverence. When this pact is not kept with the animal's spirit, nature finds its own way to rebalance the picture, often with dire consequences to the hunter and his family. This story concerns the family of a great Diomede seal netter, who was known to always keep a full cache of dried meat beneath the floor of his home. He had a wife, two sons, and a dog.

One winter, the straits froze solid with ice. No fishing or hunting was possible. The people of Little Diomede began to starve. The cache beneath the seal netter's home was used up. The great seal netter gradually wasted away and died. His family survived only by slowly rationing among themselves his seal nets, which were made of animal sinew.

One morning, desperate for food, the elder son set out in a cold, northerly windstorm to scavenge the shoreline for anything edible. A long way from the village, he came upon a strange conical-shaped object on the ice. He tapped it with his walking stick and discovered it was hollow inside. Toppling it over, he found to his amazement that there was a hole beneath it, a hole that revealed another world below the water. Curiosity led the boy to lean too far into

SELAWIK GIRL. E. S. CURTIS, SPECIAL COLLECTIONS DIVISION, UNIVERSITY OF WASHINGTON LIBRARIES, NEGATIVE NO. NA 2055.

the hole, and he lost his balance, falling far below.

Landing dazed at the bottom, he heard the sound of someone chopping and followed the noise to a house. Just outside the door stood Sea-Man chopping wood. Sea-Man invited the boy inside, and his wife offered him whale meat, which he ate voraciously.

Sea-Man, rightly judging that the whale meat had been the first meal the boy had had in a long time, inquired about the people of the boy's village. "How are they getting along?" Sea-Man asked.

"We have no food," the boy replied. "The people are very thin and worn. My father starved to death."

Noticing his tired face, Sea-Man invited the boy to spend the night and promised that he would help him return home in the morning.

The youth gratefully stayed the night, but he had difficulty falling to sleep, worrying about how he would manage to get home to his village so far above. In the morning, Sea-Man asked, "How many people are there in your home?"

"There are only my mother, my brother, and our dog."

The wife then gave the boy a long strip of whale blubber and meat. Sea-Man asked, "When your father was alive, how did he hunt?"

"He always hunted seals with nets," said the boy.

Sea-Man gave the boy a staff with an ice pick on one end and a scoop on the other. "Your village is surrounded by solid ice, so you cannot hunt or fish. Take this staff. At home, go outside the village, out of sight, and strike the ice with

the pick. Something will happen. Spread the net, and if you get something you cannot kill, touch its head with the stick. Do not take this pick home with you. Bury it under the snow near where you make the holes."

Then Sea-Man produced a top as wide as and taller than a man. The boy, pick in hand, grasped the top's handle, and the host spun the top around, which rose in the air and glided through the hole in the ice. Once above the ice, the young man secured himself and dropped the top back through the hole.

When he returned home, his family were weeping for him; they thought he was lost or dead. He removed his parka and cut a small piece from the whale meat. It swelled until it was large enough to provide a huge meal for the entire family. Before long, they became well and healthy again.

One evening, the boy took the pick and a net and walked far to the north of the village. He chose a good place, and struck the ice with his pick. It cracked and broke into a wide space of open water.

He scooped ice away from the hole and set his net. As soon as he felt it drag, he pulled, hauling in a large seal, which he killed by touching the pick to its head. All night, the boy netted, until the ice nearby was piled with seal.

After hiding his pick near the hole, he went back for the whole village, and all of the people—even those on Big Diomede—feasted and were soon strong again. The youth became a

SILUK, DIOMEDE. E. S. CURTIS, SPECIAL COLLECTIONS DIVISION, UNIVERSITY OF WASHINGTON LIBRARIES, NEGATIVE NO. NA 2027.

good hunter. He kept his cache filled and gave away much meat to others. One night, he went to find his pick, and it was gone. There were no tracks—it had disappeared without trace.

The young man returned to the world below to consult Sea-Man. Hearing the story, Sea-Man brought out his sealskin hunting bag. From it he drew a long piece of seaweed, which he flung to the floor. The seaweed hit the floor and instantly turned into a boat crew with eight men at the ready. Next, Sea-Man called for his wife to bring him his broad-bladed steering paddle.

Set in the paddle's handle, which was on a swivel and could be turned in any direction, were two eyes. Sea-Man asked the paddle what had happened to the pick. "Is the person who stole my ice pick in any of these villages?"

"No."

"Did Sun take it?"

"No."

"Did Moon take it?"

"Yes."

Sea-Man told the young man he would have to recover the ice pick himself. He gave him the boat and its crew to carry him to the moon. "When you get there," Sea-Man instructed, "ask for the pick. If Moon-Man refuses to give it back, let my paddle steal his wife and bring her here."

The young man, paddle in hand, climbed into the boat, and the crew took their places. They paddled up, through the hole, and then rose in the air toward the moon. When they arrived on the moon, he saw a house in the distance and walked toward it. Moon-Man was outside the door, chopping wood. The young man confronted him. "I have come for my ice pick."

"I did not take it," Moon-Man said. "I have everything of my own that I need."

"I am told by the man who lives on the sea bottom that you took it," the young man retorted.

Moon-Man steadfastly denied any knowledge of the ice pick. Before the young man returned to the boat, he threw his paddle into the entranceway of the house. Moon-Man's wife, who heard the clatter, rose and bent over the paddle. She saw its eyes staring at her. She poked it with her foot. Her foot stuck to the paddle. Panicking, she kicked it with her other foot, but it too became fast to the paddle. She lost her balance and fell to the floor. The paddle picked her up and bore her to the boat. The crew quickly returned them to earth. The youth went home alone, while the crew, the paddle, and Moon-Man's wife went to the sea bottom.

Near midnight, the young man was awakened by someone striking the smokehole. The voice of Moon-Man echoed down. "I have brought your ice pick. Return my wife to me."

The young man refused. "Find her yourself," he called.

"I will pay you anything for her. I will make you the strongest man in the village," Moon-Man offered, but the youth refused.

"I will make you the best hunter on earth."

Again, the reply was, "No, you must find your wife yourself."

"Come out and see what I will give you," said Moon-Man enticingly.

The young man grew curious enough to get dressed and go outside. Moon-Man said, "I will give you this ivory hook. With it you can reach out and pull in anything in the world that you wish. I will show you the man from Big Diomede who used to visit your father."

Moon-Man reached over to Big Diomede with the hook and dragged back a man who was still sleeping. "This man often came to your father's house," he said. "You too can do this. I shall put this man back where I got him."

The youth accepted the ivory hook and took back his ice pick. Then he guided Moon-Man down through the hole in the ice to the sea bottom so that he could retrieve his wife.

When Sea-Man saw them coming, he rushed out of his house and beat both Moon-Man and the youth severely. "What did Moon-Man pay you to make you bring him here?" he asked the young man. "I told you to refuse all offers from him."

Sea-Man then stopped the beating. Moon-Man said, "I gave him an ivory hook with a supernatural power. If you will return my wife to me, I shall give you this spear."

Moon-Man demonstrated that the spear also had supernatural power. "Look over there. There is a polar bear," he said. His spear reached far away and touched the bear. The bear fell over dead. Pacified by this generous offer, and greatly desiring such a fine weapon, Sea-Man made the trade. "But," he said, "you will have to get above on your own."

Moon-Man declared, "Watch us! Something will take us back."

With his words, a ladder appeared that reached far above the hole in the ice. Moon-Man and his wife, dragging the young man by his wrists, climbed. On the earth's surface, before leaving for the moon, Moon-Man said, "Oh, youth, now I am pleased. I have my wife again. I gave you the ivory hook. Whenever you want anything, no matter how far away, reach out with the hook and you will get it."

The young man became a great hunter, like his father, and he married a woman from Big Diomede Island. But one day, he caught a mouse, a tiny mouse, by its tail just as it was about to dive into its hole. Cruelly, he skinned the mouse alive and flung down its body in sport. Mouse, in great pain, ran home to her young ones, who were so frightened to see her bleeding that they began whimpering. That night, Mouse told her offspring, "That man was helped by Moon-Man and the man down below."

Mouse painfully dragged herself upright and went to the young man's home when all were asleep. Across the entrance, she raised her raw paws over her head and slapped them so hard on the floor that the family all arose and looked at her. Instantly, the young man and his wife and their entire family became old people, doddering, wrinkled, near the point of death. Mouse ran over their bodies gleefully and scampered through the entrance and then up the slope behind the village. The man and his entire family slowly followed Mouse over the mountain. No one ever knew what happened to them after that.

Kingigan

The Ancient Link Between East and West

➤

At the shortest distance between the Siberia and Alaska mainlands in the Bering Strait, the Seward Peninsula juts out like an arrowhead pointing the way back to an ancient land link that in Ice Age history connected these two vast continents.

At the tip of this coastal arrow lies the village traditionally known as Kingigan, today called Wales. Kingigan was once the largest of the Bering Sea Eskimo villages, an ancient native trading center that was noted on the earliest Russian maps existing of the Greatland. Even in the year 1880, Kingigan numbered no less than 400 people. It was here and on the Diomede islands that Yankee whaling ships had recruited native crews and also had spread many diseases of civilization. By the time Curtis came ashore here forty-seven years later, contact with whites and in particular the lethal 1917 influenza epidemic had reduced the population to 165. In 1927 the missionaries were wresting control of Kingigan, and the deep social problems of a conquered race were already upon the people.

Kingigan rested on the southern terminus of a gently curving sandy beach that extends northeastly for more than 100 miles to Kotzebue Sound. The tundra flat behind Kingigan extends to Shishmaref Inlet and is broken by many shallow lagoons that are the breeding and feeding grounds for thousands of waterfowl.

Just south of Kingigan, the sandy shoreline ends abruptly in the high, stony Cape Prince of Wales, where from the top, on a clear day, you can see Siberia. Stationed like silent sentinels at intervals up the seaward face of the cape are the stone men, *inukshuk,* who are found in watchful positions guarding ancient Eskimo territories throughout the Arctic.

These stone figures were artfully piled from various shaped rocks in such a way as to resemble Eskimos in parkas, half crouched with arms outstretched in the classic alert-and-prepared position. Enemies approaching Kingigan from the Bering Sea, such as the dreaded Siberian Chukchi Eskimo, would believe the men of the cape to be ever alert and ready. Not wishing to

risk heavy losses in open battle, the enemy raiders would turn back.

In earlier times, the village of Kingigan was said to have been divided into three parts, with the northern end separated by a river that has since filled in and the southern section divided from the other two by a small stream. The families of the three sections held a sense of bitterness and rivalry toward one another, and very little socializing took place among the factions.

Legends speak of a medicine man in the northern portion of the village who conjured a dense fog one night, so that his people might be concealed by it and slip away unnoticed. These people were said to have migrated to the Point Barrow region, where place and family names of Cape Prince of Wales origin can still be found.

At the time of the Curtis party's visit, Kingigan consisted of two settlements, each with its own men's house. The sense of aloofness between the two parts of the village was still evident, though relationships apparently were not quite as strained as in centuries past.

The villagers were primarily whalers, but from the ocean and its tributaries they also took walrus, sea lions, seals, and fish; from the ice fields they hunted polar bears and white foxes; and the land yielded birds, eggs, and fur-bearing mammals. For all the diversity in Kingigan's food supply, however, the upper echelon of village society was defined by its whaling crews, the sturdiest and bravest men of the cape, who were regarded in a class by themselves.

They hunted the bowhead whales in spring as the majestic beasts of the deep made their way north through ice floes to the Arctic Ocean. The whaling crews, who were usually relatives of the boat owner and captain, held their posi-

tions permanently and were regarded with great respect.

Before whale hunting took place, a woman, considered to be a ceremonial member of the crew, was chosen to take part in the ceremonies. Sometimes several crews chose the same woman and held joint ceremonies in the men's house. Once the boats were fitted with new coverings, they were carried to their racks, where they were placed upside down. The chosen woman followed behind, bearing a dish of food, and took up her position beside a boat. Young village boys lined up on the opposite side of the boat, and the woman playfully threw portions of food over the boat to the children, which the boys scrambled to catch. The boats were then allowed to dry for a few days and grow taut in the elements.

Equipment was brought to the boat owner's home and repaired or replaced, and all wooden paddles and gear were shaved with knives to give the appearance of newness. The crews dressed in new clothing and feasted and danced to drive away any evil influences that might cling to their work.

The air pokes were soaked until pliable. Then the boat owner and harpooner hiked up the cape to a hidden cache on the mountainside known only to them. Here, harpoon heads and points, talismans, and supernatural charms were kept during the off-season. These trusted and sacred objects were taken to the boat when it was ready to be launched, and they were placed in various parts of the craft, attached to the frame, on pokes, paddles, and harpoons. No two crews had similar objects, nor did they place them in exactly the same way. Knowledge of the cache, of the spirit-power objects, and of their proper usage was carefully passed on from father to son.

The 1917 influenza epidemic so decimated the village, elders and youngsters alike, that many of these caches were lost forever. Curtis's assistant, Eastwood, discovered one such cache while he was walking the cape. It contained several stuffed bird skins, which had disintegrated; a wolf and a fox skull, each including the jaw-bones; a caribou hoof and shin bone; a wolf claw with two stones lashed to it; a headband with a blue bead in the center; and a talismans box made from a tree branch with a sinew handle attached. Inside the box was a pebble, a blue bead, a rolled parchment, and several beads wrapped in intestinal parchment. Sewn skin bags containing dried whale meat were hung from the cache by long sinew belts. Other objects included a harpoon rest for the bow of a boat, a large wooden ladle, and a wooden bird, whose belly was hollowed out to hold spare harpoon points.

To touch these objects if they did not belong to you was to invite dire consequences, and the villagers treated Eastwood with suspicion when he brought back a carved harpoon that bore the mark of a family who had died during the plague. At that time, the harpoons were in disuse and small bomb guns were being employed, but their magic was still considered private and powerful.

After a boat paddle was placed by its owner on the shore ice, a full night followed of singing the ceremonial songs of the boat owner. In the morning, the boat and gear were carried to shore. The woman brought out a dish of food and threw the food over the boat to the village boys. She made a mark of ash on her forehead. The boat was righted, all the gear was placed properly, and while the owner sang, the boat was dragged to the ice. Everyone sang together a prayer for the hunt. As the men passed the paddle placed in the ice the night before, the harpooner seized it and set it in the bow. The boat was carried to the ice edge, where the crew took their places. The boat owner tied a pair of animal ears onto the blade of the paddle and lightly brushed the surface of the water, so that the whales would not hear their approach.

The boat was launched and allowed to drift out a ways. The crew sang, and the woman, left standing on the ice, sang back to them. The boat was put about suddenly and headed toward her, while the harpooner motioned as if to spear the woman. She scattered ashes about to drive away the evil spirits and ran home without looking back. She would remain inside and fast until a whale was killed or the crew returned.

When a whale was killed, a designated member of the crew wrapped a piece of its skin and blubber around his shoulders as proof and ran home to the woman. She distributed the meat among the families of the crew or crews.

Later, after the whale was dragged out on the shore ice, a messenger, carrying a piece of the whale's fluke on a small spear, was sent to the woman. She cut the fluke into small strips and cooked the meat, then it was placed in a new pot and carried around to the villagers. This signaled the crew's families to make ready for the butchering. The woman, dressed in her finest attire, was taken to the ice by dog team, where she sang and danced in praise of the hunters. The boat owner replied with dancing and singing. The woman distributed some of the fresh meat to the crew, who immediately ate it. To refresh the whale spirit's thirst, she poured fresh water over its blowhole and also presented the whale with a hair from her parka. The crew packed the boat gear to the village. The pokes were placed on the platform caches, and lines were strung on the boat racks to dry. Then the crews slept, because the cutting took a full two days of steady labor.

During the whaling season, children were encouraged to play games imitating their elders' activities in the whale hunt, but after the hunting was over, the children had to play the games of the following season, and so on throughout the year. In this way, the people taught their chil-

ON KOTZEBUE SOUND. E. S. CURTIS, SPECIAL COLLECTIONS DIVISION, UNIVERSITY OF WASHINGTON LIBRARIES, NEGATIVE NO. NA 1980.

dren early the rhythms and migratory cycles of the animals, and never to base their survival on any one aspect of hunting or gathering.

In the early spring, when food was likely to be scarce, the men moved out to the edge of the ice, where they built snow or ice barricades to hide them from their quarry. They sat on their air pokes and peeped through holes on the lookout for seals. As the animals came up, they were harpooned and hauled in by the harpoon line. The seals were seen as this season's life-sustaining gift, and unsuccessful hunters and their families could ask the more fortunate for a share of the game. Since generosity was the mark of a great hunter and his own guarantee of future bounty,

it sometimes happened that the hunter was left with only the head and stomach for himself.

Seals were also hunted from kayaks, and the hunter and his wife would conduct a ceremony similar to that of the more elaborate whaling ritual. She would mark herself with ash and become the seal, and he would pass by in his kayak and pretend to harpoon her before setting out on the hunt.

Sea lions, hair seals, and walrus were caught when conditions were favorable. Polar bears, which in myth flew down from the stars, were hunted on the ice with spears and bows. Amazingly, the men also hunted the polar bears by boat. The harpoon was thrown at the hindquarters of the bear, and the crew kept the line taut by backing the boat away from the bear. This kept the lethal forepaws and jaws away from the boat. Heavy stones on loops were then slid down the line, until the bear sank into the water from the weight and drowned. Dozens of

WHALING FLEET, PORT CLARENCE (SHIPS IN HARBOR, NATIVE TENTS ON SHORE). E. S. CURTIS, 1899, HARRIMAN ALASKA EXPEDITION ALBUM, SPECIAL COLLECTIONS DIVISION, UNIVERSITY OF WASHINGTON LIBRARIES, NEGATIVE NO. NA 2125.

Eskimos on a Whaler

stories and legends about the polar bears attest to the fact that in face-offs between polar bears and men, often the bears won and the men didn't return home.

During the first part of May, the eider ducks, revered for the warmth and waterproof qualities of their skins, arrived in large flocks on the edge of the shore ice. The Kingigan caught them with bolas, which were thrown from boats with a seal bladder attached to the handles so that the birds would not be lost in the water.

Crabs were caught a little later in the spring and were found only in a limited area between Cape Prince of Wales and a few miles southward. The people used dip nets, with a hoop made of horn. The weighted nets were baited

ESKIMOS ON A WHALER, PORT CLARENCE. E. S. CURTIS, 1899, HARRIMAN ALASKA EXPEDITION ALBUM, SPECIAL COLLECTIONS DIVISION, UNIVERSITY OF WASHINGTON LIBRARIES, NEGATIVE NO. NA 2124.

with bits of blubber or fish and lowered into deep water, to be drawn up at intervals and the catch removed.

Summer brought the caribou to the Seward Peninsula, and hunters would go inland to a lake. Runners would round up the caribou and stampede them toward the lake, driving them between two lines of men whose shouts and gestures frightened the animals into the water. Once in the lake, they were speared by men in kayaks, while people stationed around the shore

prevented the animals from escaping. The meat was dried before it was hauled back to Kingigan.

After the caribou hunting was finished, poorer families remained along the coast, where they would fish as far south as Teller. Others who could afford large skin boats would travel to Siberia, the Diomedes, and Kotzebue to trade. Often the Diomede islanders visited and traded for land items before the villagers had scattered along the coast. Along the Chukotsk Peninsula in Siberia, they traded portions of the caches for iron to use in making weapons and for furs such as beaver, deer, fox, otter, and wolverine. In Kotzebue, they traded for caribou, fox, muskrat, and squirrel.

In autumn, when storms begin to brew in the Bering Sea, the summer's catch was placed in caches for storage, houses were repaired and new ones built, and nets were set out for beluga, sea lion, and seal when the water was cold and the nets would not rot. The nets were visited every day and were kept out until the ice formed.

Boat crews of about ten men took larger nets to a protected area around the cape, safe from the quick-blowing storms, where they dipped for whatever could be caught. Villagers reported that as many as fifty seals could be hauled in on a good night.

After the fall storms, clams blown up on the beach were collected, and the women would travel south to make pots and lamps from a clay found near Tin City. Apparently, this site was also lost after the 1917 flu epidemic.

Families moved into the village in early winter, and ritualized visiting was held. The men's house was opened, and each family brought in its stone lamp and set it in its place in the house. Food was brought in for feasting, games were

played, stories of the hunt were told, and the crews danced and sang. The songs and dances of each family and records of lives and hunts were in this way handed down from generation to generation. The old men, young unmarried men, and boys lived and slept in the men's house, where they worked on sleds, weapons, and implements of all kinds and received food brought in by the women.

The more important ceremonies at Cape Prince of Wales were connected to the hunting of whales, walrus, and seals, and included the Messenger Feast. Other ceremonies surrounded the customs of childbirth and the giving of names. As soon as a child's navel had healed, the child was given a name of a relative to keep the name in the family. When the birth occurred during the winter, the mother had to limit her diet to one form of food, usually seal meat, and refrain from drinking water until the following spring. It was believed that this regimen would cause a male child to grow up to be a good hunter and a girl baby to become skilled in womanly pursuits.

In Kingigan, as elsewhere in the Bering Strait, the first bird a boy killed was carefully skinned and a feast was held. The boy's head was shaved to denote his passage as a hunter among men, and the bird skin and weapons were displayed on the wall of the men's house. After the feast, the bird skin and the bow and arrows used in the hunt were burned behind the village to signify that the spirit of the bird could return to its nest. The boy, by thus honoring and releasing the bird's spirit, would be aided in becoming a good hunter. When little girls first ventured forth with their mothers to pick berries and gather plants, they presented their first attempts at gathering to the older people of the village.

Marriage was a little more complicated to achieve in Kingigan than on some of the Bering Sea islands. A youth, who had first proved himself by killing both a sea lion and a seal, had to gain the consent of both of the girl's parents, then provide his chosen with a complete outfit of new clothing. If the girl accepted the clothing, the youth would have to hunt and provide meat for her parents for some time in order to gain their respect as a good provider. If the girl refused the offer of marriage, the clothing had to be returned. It was also returned in the event of divorce, which was decided upon by mutual agreement or if either party was unfaithful. Murder was accepted as common punishment for adulterers.

Death was surrounded by sacred ritual, from dressing the body in a new set of clothes to hoisting it through the smokehole so that all sickness and evil would pass out of the house with it. The relatives would then bear the body, along with food and the person's utensils, tools, and weapons, to a suitable spot on the mountain. The body was laid with the head facing south, and a grave board was placed beneath, on each side, and on the top and was weighted down with stones. Possessions were placed atop the rocks. Before the family left the grave site, they built a fire and burned a pungent herb called *iksudit,* purifying themselves by rubbing their bodies in the smoke.

Upon returning to the house, the smokehole was closed, the room was heated, and the family bathed. Each member rubbed his or her body with a stone. In this way, evil and sickness might pass from their bodies into the stone, and they would be further hardened against sickness and evil. If the deceased was a man, the family had to remain indoors, performing no work, for four days, while relatives came in with food. If it was a woman who had died, the mourning period lasted five days. The men could not hunt, nor women fish, until the next new moon. Upon returning from their first hunting or fishing trip, the men and women had to bite a stone to prevent their teeth from falling out. This period of mourning was observed to prevent the dead person's spirit, as it wandered about the village, from doing harm, such as keeping game and fish from migrating through the area.

A year later, the family carried food to the grave to scatter. A feast was held, and the relatives who had carried the body were invited. It was believed that the spirit of the dead had by this time gone to a village somewhere on the mountainside, and would be present at the feast and eat the food on the grave. If the deceased was a good hunter, the bones of the whales he killed, his polar bear heads, and his kayak were placed on the grave at this time.

If the spirit refused to leave and lingered in the village, making its presence known by doing mischief and harm to the people, it was a sign that some possession or article the spirit desired had been left in the house. The family in that case had to consult a medicine man, who found out what the desired article was and informed the family. By placing the item on the grave, the spirit would be appeased and go to the village of the dead, where it would meet and live with its ancestors.

LEGENDS

Of Whales and Men, and Intermarriage with Polar Bears

➤

Most of the stories attached to the Kingigan people were whale tales, of spiritually enlightened villagers who became whales in order to help the cape hunters better understand the animals they sought.

Such is the case with the story of four men who drifted out to sea on an ice floe. They were carried to the Land of Whales, where the whale spirits gathered in a large men's house. All of the wounded whales came there, and the dead were laid away behind the house. The four men lived with the whales, eating shrimp and often, when they needed meat, cutting slices from the dead whales. After eating the meat, they had to live away from the whale people for four days.

Some whale spirits wore new parkas; they had been killed by hunters who had performed the whale ceremonies properly and with respect. Spirits with old parkas, on the other hand, had been killed by men who had been careless concerning the rituals.

The men learned that in the spring, two white whales, belugas, were sent out as scouts from the Land of Whales to report on conditions, to find out which villages were clean and whose houses were in disrepair or who was burning rotten fuel.

The whales chose their route north based on the reports of the belugas because whales avoided places that were unclean and went farther out to sea to skirt a village if the dead were improperly buried. The men were informed that as the whales were preparing for their northward migration, the hunters should be about the business of overhauling their gear and gathering animal talismans of fox, wolf, or any other four-legged creature. The whales told the men that the boats to be used in the whale hunt became animated the night before the launch. The boats walked on animal legs represented by their owners' talismans to the Land of Whales. Those craft that succeeded in reaching the whale land on their own and returning by the next morning would carry their owners and crews on a successful hunt.

After the four humans had been fully instructed by the whale spirits, they returned to

Kingigan and told everyone what they had learned. Since that time, people have been very careful to keep the village clean, to keep all whaling equipment neat and in working order, and to observe burial rites faithfully. With these acts, the whale spirits are pleased and a successful whaling season is assured.

➤

Sometimes, Kingigan stories centered around men or women who went to live with the animals and found their new lives in the natural world too good to leave behind. Though these people never returned to the land of humans, they often increased the power of a village and kinship to its prey.

The man who married a polar bear is a long and intricate tale that reveals much about the quirky characteristics of polar bears. A man who was a good hunter lived with his mother, who was growing elderly and wanted him to marry so that she would have a good helper.

The man could not find anyone in the village whom he wanted to marry, nor did he know of anyone in other villages. One time he went out hunting on the shore ice, jumped on an ice floe, and drifted far out to sea. He spied a woman, dressed in a beautiful white parka trimmed with bear fur, playing with a ball of tanned sealskin. As the ice floe he was standing on grew near hers, his curiosity overtook him and he called out, "Why do you play ball on this ice floe? Why don't you play on land? Where did you come from?"

She turned casually toward him and answered, "I belong out here. I play here because I like to."

"Are you married?" asked the man.

"No, I have never been with men," she answered.

"I have never married or been with a woman," he said. "Will you marry me?"

The woman agreed, but she warned her new mate that the time would come when trouble would separate them, because his mother would say unkind things to her.

He led his new wife back to the village and privately drew his mother aside to caution her not to say an unkind word to the woman.

"You have followed my wishes in choosing a daughter-in-law," his mother assured him. "I shall never use harsh words toward her."

A baby boy was born to the couple, and the old woman raised him. The old woman carefully watched her daughter-in-law as she went about her duties, and was disgusted at how the younger woman always nibbled on pieces of blubber and licked up the oil when she cut meat.

Finally one day, the old woman could hold her tongue no longer. "Why does your mother always eat pieces of blubber and lick up oil when she cuts up meat?" the old woman asked her grandson. "I think she must be a polar bear."

Hearing these words, the wife wept. Soon, she dried her tears and filled the lamps purposefully, because she knew she would soon separate from her husband. She pretended nothing was wrong when her husband came back from hunting. When he finally asked her if everything was all right, she averted her gaze and refused to answer.

In the morning, when her husband arose, she remained in bed. He asked her to get up, but she turned her back to him. Again he asked her what was wrong, but he was met with hostile silence. At her refusal to answer, he stomped out of the house.

The wife and her son dressed and ran to the shore, where they fled north along the beach until they reached a rocky point. When they stepped onto the shore ice, their feet and hands grew fur and claws and became bear paws. After

ESKIMO CHILDREN, PORT CLARENCE. E. S. CURTIS, 1899, HARRIMAN ALASKA EXPEDITION ALBUM, SPECIAL COLLECTIONS DIVISION, UNIVERSITY OF WASHINGTON LIBRARIES, NEGATIVE NO. NA 2120.

a long walk, they reached the floe ice. They jumped onto the floe ice, and mother and son were transformed into polar bears.

When the man returned from hunting, his mother told him his family had left him. Snatching his weapons, he headed out to where the tracks led out over the shore ice. He knew then that they had become polar bears. Their tracks showed that they were traveling slowly,

the mother going ahead and waiting for her son to catch up.

The trail became fresher. He saw the dark vapor of their breaths rising in the still air ahead, and then he saw the two polar bears. Before he could catch up to them, they slipped into the open water, the mother swimming fast, holding her son close to her. The man ran along the shore ice in hopes of intercepting them, and he saw the spot where they eventually emerged. Picking up their trail again, he followed for a long distance until he came to two large villages.

He followed his wife's and son's tracks to the men's house in the first village. He waited outside, and soon his son came out. "You have followed us here!" his son said accusingly.

The man told the boy to fetch his wife. She refused to believe that any human could have followed them that far. Her father, an old polar bear, spoke. "What the boy says may be true, because humans sometimes travel far. Daughter, go out and see."

Seeing her husband, she asked, "Why did you come here? Your mother does not like me. You must return to your own village, because no humans can live here."

He refused to leave her, telling her passionately that he would stay, even if he were to lose his life because of it.

He went inside to meet his father-in-law, who was impressed that the man had traveled so far and fast to reach the land of the polar bears.

"But you have not yet met my sons, who are out hunting," the old man warned him. "If my eldest son is angry, you will lose your life. He will enter first. As he comes up through the entrance, throw a bead in his teeth and he will be pleased. Then he will not kill you."

Outside, bears were approaching. Growling and gnashing their teeth, one muttered that he smelled a human. The other cried, "Why did our father let a human enter our house?"

The man waited just inside the entrance, and when the eldest son ducked his head in, the man flung the bead between the bear's teeth.

START OF WHALE HUNT, CAPE PRINCE OF WALES.

E. S. Curtis, Special Collections Division, University of Washington Libraries, Negative No. NA 2031.

The eldest son's head disappeared, and in a moment he reappeared wearing the bead in a headband. Then all the sons entered. There were so many of them and they were so big that they filled the benches, their shoulders touching. They were glad to see their sister, greeted her husband buoyantly, and roughhoused joyfully with the little boy. Yet when all of the bears went to sleep, the man was kept awake by their constant growling and snoring in their sleep.

The next morning, the old man arose and told his sons to treat their brother-in-law well, because he would always remain with them. He became well liked in the village and known as a good hunter, and he told the bears much about the human beings from Kingigan who hunted them.

The neighboring village, however, was suspicious of having a human being living in their midst, and they frequently drew the man out in attempts to get the best of him. Once, wearing the skin of his father-in-law, he helped his village win in a difficult physical competition with the adjacent village. In the spring, his father-in-law announced a contest to see which village could bring in the first seal. He gave the man his skin and told him to wear it "because humans are slower hunters than polar bears."

Both villages spread out on the ice looking for seal holes. The human found an old one and cleared it off. He could see an animal swimming just below the surface. He flipped it out, and it turned out to be a big hair seal. All his polar bear brothers threw their heads back and yelled in triumph. They curved up their tails and proudly trotted home on the tips of their claws.

The old father smiled and nodded his approval. "I always won while hunting and brought home the first seal," he said. "Now all the games are over and that village will never bother you again."

Since that time, the human hunter has lived with the polar bears.

EPILOGUE

Restoring Balance in an Unbalanced World

⟩

Though men no longer marry polar bears, traditional Inupiat and Yupik stories and legends, maskmaking, dollmaking, and beautiful ivory and skin work have miraculously survived 100 years of modern American civilization.

The Russians, the whalers, the traders, the gold seekers, the missionaries, the salmon canners, the soldiers, the government planners, and the big oil drillers have all imposed themselves on Eskimo life and lands, but none have extinguished the remarkable spirit of the people.

Despite the problems Alaska natives face—and there are many associated with oppression and the slow erosion of cultural identity—the very fact that many of the young people still know something of their past, still honor close family ties, and still in many communities seek their elders' advice is credit to the endurance of their ancient communal heritage.

The old ways tenuously cling to life in the artistry of traditional Yupik maskmakers such as John Kailukiak of Toksook Bay, yet it is a fragile survival. He says people in his area don't know whether to return to making masks, because of masks' association with shamanism and magic. "There are conflicts with the churches," he said. "The churches are pretty closed minded about it. They think it's evil, I guess. But if they'd take the chance to listen, really study it, I think they'd find out different."

Masks were created and worn in order to relate the stories of hunts, represent the animals or fish the people were connected to spiritually, or provide a form of animated entertainment meant to produce laughter.

"During the days of the missionaries coming out," Kailukiak related, "they really were against the masks. They thought it was idolatry, and I guess they missed the whole concept of the masks. That was pretty sad, because they stopped that real fine art. The original purpose for those masks is pretty much gone. They were not always meant to be evil."

Masked dancers once moved in the light and shadows of ceremonial fires, evoking a spirit world where men and animals were one entity.

Today the masks are most often seen hung beneath track lighting in Alaskan art galleries. Yet the spirit masks speak through time.

In new shapes and forms, the masks also speak to the future of the original inhabitants of Alaska. In 1978 an Alaska Native Maskmaking Workshop was founded at University of Alaska–Fairbanks Native Arts Center. This brought together six master artists from around the state.

Eight years later, the Alaskameut Exhibit had grown to include forty contemporary and traditional masks, and the number of artists participating in the workshop had nearly doubled. Well-known maskmaker-artist James Schoppert said the artists were drawn together for one purpose: to create. "The materials for the creations varied considerably," he related. "There was spruce root and driftwood from Nelson Island, whalebone from Shishmaref, and full-moon hubcaps from the streets of Seattle." The 1986 workshop crossed cultural boundaries, Schoppert said, "creating something bold and new."

The flow of artistic energy and the sharing of ideas between old and young maskmakers—traditional and contemporary in style—are slowly helping to revive a dying art. Among the artists there is hope that the masks will find a new life inside their own cultures and a new understanding among non-natives.

In the old days, Inupiak Harvey Pootoogooluk collected bones and baleen from the dead whales that washed ashore during their annual Arctic migration through the Bering Sea. Now the Shishmaref artist buys the baleen from Anchorage, but his carvings still manifest his love for the land of his ancestors.

The work of traditional maskmakers like Kailukiak and Charley Post mirrors their rich Yupik heritage. Both carvers are Eskimo hunters who collect their artistic materials, such as natural pigments, feathers, ivory, and driftwood, from their surroundings.

Others, like Joseph Senungetuk, an Inupiak originally from Wales, Alaska, who now resides in Anchorage, and Fred Anderson, an Aleut who divides his time between Anchorage and his village home of Naknek, seek to make strong political statements in their art.

"I was a spectator at some of the Wales dances, celebrations of successful polar bear hunts," Senungetuk recalled. "I have watched traditional native women's dances. They were just beginning to die out when I was very young, six or seven years old."

Ever since his family first came into contact with white men and, particularly, fundamentalist missionaries, traditional life has been disrupted. Senungetuk has yearned for a rediscovery of the ceremonies, songs, dances, music, language, and oral storytelling traditions of his people.

"We're terribly stereotyped right now as native artists," Senungetuk said. "Our effectiveness is hurt by the stereotyping as to what we do and how we do it and where we display and where we sell our work. It's all thought of as normal, but if you look at it very closely, the stereotyping is still very abnormal."

On the far side of contemporary masks, Lawrence Beck, who was born and raised in Seattle, finds his treasured materials in auto supply stores and rusty junkyards. Beck has completed an entire series of spirit masks made out of salad forks, oilcan spouts, hubcaps, and spatulas. Forks become eagle claws, oilcan spouts become walrus tusks, and punk walrus peer out of snow tires.

With continued support for the workshops, and the maskmakers' diligence to carve out a distinctive niche for their art, the songs of the spirit world may yet endure.

Whereas maskmaking was and is a male-dominated artistic realm, Eskimo women have for generations passed down the arts of dollmaking and skin sewing from mother to daughter. Their handwork is renowned throughout the North for its exquisite quality and elaborate detail.

Sharon Cloud, an Inupiak dollmaker turned contemporary artist who lives in Chugiak, has been known to spend weeks hand molding and sewing the soles of tiny two-inch-high mukluks to be used on her dolls from the *oogruk*—the heavy spotted seal gut—only to decide she didn't like them and start over using squirrel skin. Sharon's dolls are museum quality, from their wood-carved faces with inset ivory and baleen

JUKUK, NUNIVAK ISLAND. *Christian name: Lena Wesley. Lip decorations: ivory labrets. Waterproof gut parka.* E. S. Curtis, Special Collections Division, University of Washington Libraries, Negative No. NA 1991. _____

eyes to their handsewn Eskimo fur parkas and leggings. Each one takes up to six months of labor, no two are alike, and she has steadfastly refused commissioned work.

"They are bigger than what I am," she said of her dolls. "I don't know where it comes from—maybe it is all your ancestry coming together. The first four dolls I made look just like someone I know."

Her third Eskimo doll, a man dressed in a muskrat parka, was completed in 1987, and she

ESKIMO IN SKIN KAYAK. E. S. Curtis, 1928, PCA 49-1, Alaska State Library. _____

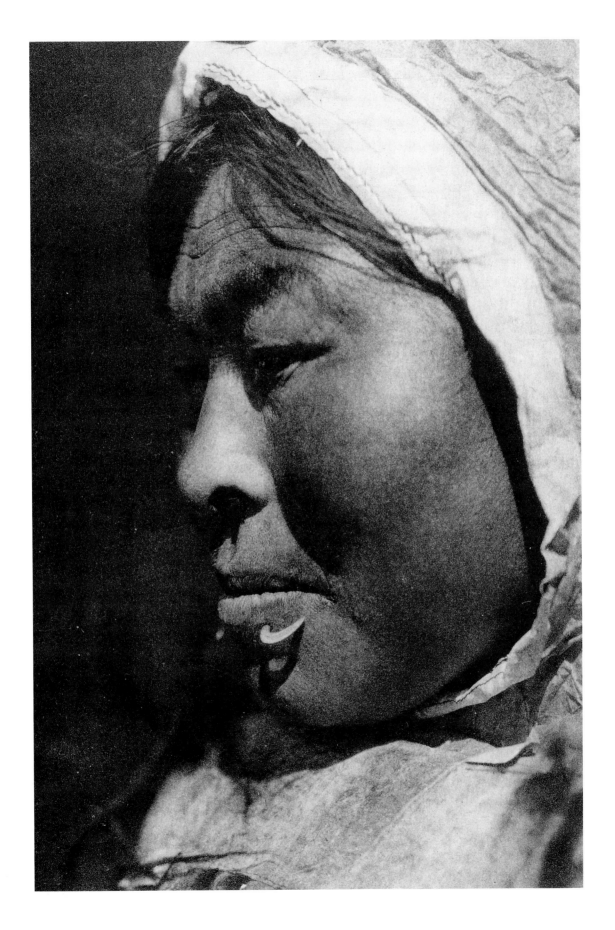

entered it in the Alaska State Fair competition. It won first place and grand champion. She sold it to a doll collector from Iowa.

"At first you think that once you've made one or two dolls, you've seen it all. But it's not like that," she explained. "Each one opens another door."

In the beginning stages of her career, Sharon's mother gave her pieces of coyote and beaver fur—expensive pieces that helped Sharon develop a taste for creating a higher-quality doll. One of her dolls, which was purchased by the Dillingham Hospital, was a fierce shaman with piercing eyes and an elaborate ivory and cottonwood bark mask, patterned after Sharon's grandfather. Like all of Sharon's dolls, the shaman received its spiritual link to the past and its name—Elakoak—from her mother.

"The shaman is named after my grandfather, who started into a shaman's trance but was interrupted halfway and never completed the transition," Sharon said.

Sharon turned the telling of her grandfather's story over to her mother, Lillian Ingram, an able storyteller with bright eyes who sat near Sharon in a chair, hands folded serenely in her lap. The older woman smiled, and then she sat very still.

"I think it was up in Shishmaref, when my father was not very old," related Mrs. Ingram. "Grandpa's wife was a troublemaker, a complainer, and finally the village council members invited Grandpa to come to the men's house. He went through the tunnel, and his head came up in that room, and all five council members shot him." (The villagers apparently had decided that the only way to push the troublemaker out of the village was to kill her husband first.)

"The village council controlled the harmony of the village," Sharon explained. "The council was afraid that if she and her son stayed on in the village after that happened, they would eventually seek revenge for my great-grandfather's death."

The old woman picked up the thread of the story again. In haste, the widow and her son fled Shishmaref, fearing that the young man's life was in danger if they stayed. The family, originally from the Bering Sea coast, traveled widely, eventually settling in the western Alaska town of Dillingham, after dogsledding the distance in midwinter.

"One time we were at Dawson Creek, and my father went into a trance, a seventy-two-hour trance," Mrs. Ingram remembered. "But a dog fell through the skylight and broke the spell."

Sharon finished the story. "My mother's father became quite religious after that. He was a mail-team dog driver and a preacher, and he later passed on what the missionaries taught to him."

Sharon's shaman doll honoring the spirit of her grandfather led her to create a doll of an older Eskimo woman picking salmonberries, to honor the berry-picking passion of her great-grandmother.

"My grandmother, when she was so old, she couldn't walk or anything, but she would crawl to pick salmonberries," Mrs. Ingram said, a wide grin spreading across her weathered face.

Sharon had to carve and recarve the berry-picker's face many times, "because every time I'd start in on it, it turned out to be a younger woman's face. I wanted her face to look like she had accomplished something—you know Eskimos love picking berries."

Sharon's inspiration for her dollmaking is firmly planted in family stories, her innate respect for the earth, and a spirituality that embraces both traditional Inupiat beliefs and modern Christianity.

Most recently, she has begun to turn to painting as a medium that allows her more freedom to create what she sees, and it's fair to say Sharon sees people differently than most. She paints portraits of medicine women drumming up eagle spirits that swoop from the sky, and maskmakers with new-moon eyes being visited by Raven.

When Sharon first saw the Curtis Eskimo portraits that are reproduced in this book, she placed her finger on each one of the photographs, tracing the *inua,* or animal spirit, she saw clearly etched within the facial features of the person depicted. "Walrus," she said about one man's photo; "Seal," about another.

The spiritual link between people and animals and the natural world is still very strong in the Eskimo culture, even among middle-aged people like Sharon Cloud, who live in modern homes and yet travel back to their home villages seasonally for fishing, berry picking, and hunting activities that still involve extended family.

But there is a dangerous bear on the prowl in Alaska, a predator that turns the proud Eskimo hunter into the hunted and tears away at native family life. The polar bear was a benign adversary compared with this predator—alcoholism.

In a native counselor's handbook on the treatment of alcoholism, one Canadian Inuit elder described alcohol as a spirit who came to her people in a ceremony. She described how powerful this spirit was, because no matter how much grief it created, the people would always defend it. She emphasized how the people must respect alcohol by never underestimating its power to control.

Traditionally, the family and community were more important in native life than the individual. This sense of identity within a larger group is being undermined by the impacts of alcoholism. Today, many Eskimo families and villages are experiencing tremendous losses due to alcoholism, suicide, and family violence. In

facing and healing alcoholism, the struggle for survival among Alaska's native peoples is dependent upon their reestablishing the relationships they have traditionally had with one another, with all living things, and with the land.

In Alaska, the road to alcoholism among many native people has been one of displacement, anger, and pain, and to understand its bitter roots, one has to listen to a story.

Mary Stachelrodt is a Yupik grandmother who now lives in a modern house in Palmer, Alaska, just north of Anchorage. She was born in Bethel, inland from the Bering Sea. Her father, Nick Charles, was born on Nelson Island, which along with Nunivak Island was among the last areas along the Alaska coast to come under the influence of white people. Her father and mother were raised traditionally near Bethel and traveled to hunt and gather food on the tundra and Nelson Island.

"My dad and mom traveled in the wilderness tundra and rivers, and Mom would sometimes be alone for days in her subterranean hut while Dad was out hunting," Mary recalled. "It's a beautiful love story the way Mom tells it. The minute she'd see my dad coming, she'd get up on top of the hut and dance for him—bringing him in." Mary motioned gracefully with her hands the Eskimo sign of welcome. "Then Mom would run and hide because she was shy."

Mary's parents traveled far to trade and to search for food. It wasn't uncommon for a family to sail all the way to the Aleutian Islands to the south and Jackson Island to the north, a span of hundreds of miles, in the course of a summertime, not to mention long forays into the Alaska mainland tracking game and picking berries. "My mother lost a lot of her babies on the tundra, on the move," Mary said.

"When I was a kid, we were somewhat nomadic," she related. "We went to fish camp, we had a summer and a fall camp and a winter camp, and we traveled far. We also had a permanent home in Bethel. Respectfully, traditional people were taught to leave camp areas better than they found them. There is no evidence at all of my family ever being in those places, because my dad kept the camps up well. Life seemed very carefree and peaceful then.

"But my whole life came to an abrupt stop," Mary continued quietly, her small, expressive hands coming to rest in her lap. The Bureau of Indian Affairs declared that all native children would be assimilated into white society by attending residential schools. They were to forget their past. Leave their families. Embrace the future, the superior white way. To an Eskimo family, used to living within the rhythms of the seasons, used to teaching and including their children in every activity, used to leading physi-

cally active, subsistence-based lives, losing their children meant losing the future. "I remember we stopped going to winter camps so we could go to school in Bethel," Mary related.

Mary was punished frequently for speaking her own language. "I grew up angry," she declared, her eyes filled with sudden fire. "I grew up feeling like part of me was cheated by the intruders. When I went away to school, I missed my grandparents, as I had often lived with them for months. I went to Mass and communion. There were too many dos and don'ts. I rebelled against that. I still said my prayers, five Hail

ESKIMOS PADDLING KAYAKS. E. S. CURTIS, PCA 49-10, ALASKA STATE LIBRARY. _____

Marys, and Acts of Contrition. But I lost the basic laws of my people concerning respect, unity, and giving. I often felt that there was a gaping hole in my life after we stopped our seasonal trips to our camps."

Alcohol, unknown to her on Nelson Island, was offered by whites and other displaced, isolated native kids who were looking for a way to dull their misery.

NUNIVAK CHILDREN, DUCK-SKIN PARKAS. E. S. CURTIS, 1928, PCA 49-2, ALASKA STATE LIBRARY.

"I grew up drunk and crazy," she said. "At thirty-six I quit drinking, and I'd been drunk most of those years. The day that turned my life around happened in this very house in 1980. My two children came home and said they were leaving. They were tired of smelling the alcohol, tired of my stupor and suicide attempts. It was a shocker—it spun my life around. I didn't want to lose them."

Alcohol had wrecked Mary's first marriage. She and her second husband both were barely functioning alcoholics. They had managed for years to blanket themselves in denial, though

Mary in her most drunken stupor sometimes found herself "beg-praying to God for help. I call it beg-praying—I used to beg him for help." Mary shook her head slowly. "Something inside of me said this wasn't right, but it was hard. I knew we couldn't do it alone."

"We got into recovery at the same time," she said. "It didn't matter whether we lived or died at that point. I called AA and they twelve-stepped us. I look at it as a miracle."

Mary and her husband got sober. Over time, their children grew to respect them. And in her recovery, Mary came back to the spiritual teachings of her childhood steeped in the traditional ways. She decided she had to help others.

For the past decade, Mary has worked in the substance abuse field as a counselor, board member, clinical supervisor, and director. She is a board member of the National Native American

ESKIMO CHILDREN IN KAYAK. E. S. CURTIS, PCA 49-13, ALASKA STATE LIBRARY.

AIDS Prevention Center. She served on the Governor's Juvenile Justice Advisory Committee for five years, as well as on the Alaska Women's Commission "Leadership in Sobriety Conference" planning committee. She has provided workshops in cross-cultural training and addiction, recovery, and suicide prevention across the state of Alaska.

"I incorporate drumming, singing, smudging with purifying herbs, Eskimo dance and storytelling into the workshops," Mary says. "The workshops used to be more blood, guts, and tears, but after a while, they became more fun. Alaska native people traditionally had talking circles and purification rituals for healing. I

use a beaded eagle feather in healing circles; it is a symbol for being truthful. It takes a lot of releasing and sharing and many turns talking, telling of the pain and joy. In the talking circle our ancestors are here, watching, helping, and guiding us. To speak, one must hold the feather. It is a permission stick, like a dance stick."

Mary says that although alcoholism may seem as if it is on the rise among Native Americans, she believes the disease is only now coming to the surface to be dealt with.

"Alcoholism is like a boil. In order for the boil to heal, it comes to a pressure point, blows, then you clean it up and it heals," she explained. "It will leave a scar, but it will start healing. I think that is what is happening. It might seem like the numbers are getting bigger, but there are just more boils that need to be healed."

Now that Mary has come full circle to walk the path of a traditional Yupik healer, she is intensely involved in bringing together Indian and Eskimo peoples of the world as the coordinator for Spiritual Unity of the Tribes in Alaska, a gathering of all tribes, all peoples, that was established by the Elders of Saskatchewan in 1988 and has been held annually since 1989 in different locations in Alaska and the continental United States.

The origins of the gathering go back much further and are recounted here from the Gathering IV newsletter published in 1991, after the tribes met for the Gathering of the Eagles in the traditional territory of the Lakota Nation, the Black Hills of South Dakota.

"Many years ago," wrote Jim Walton, a Tlingit elder, "Black Elk had a vision of peace and unity among all peoples. Though years have passed, Black Elk's vision has been pondered and cherished by many, knowing that at some time the vision would be fulfilled. Sitting Bull also spoke of the time when there would be a gathering of tribes. People continued to ponder these prophesies of the great leaders and to consult the Elders regarding when and how these prophesies would be fulfilled. Many believe that the time is now."

When the gathering steering committee first began to meet, letters came in from all parts of the globe. Ales Simakou, a Byelorussian-American, wrote that his people would be very interested in a cross-cultural alcohol program. "The problem of alcoholism is a very serious one of our peoples too. . . . Your anti-alcohol experience, methods are extremely important to us."

Other native people wrote to express their sense of urgency in uniting the tribes to "bring healing to our Mother Earth" and to assist in "bringing about a glorious new age of peace and harmony based upon universal spiritual principles." Indigenous peoples who have retained a spiritual way of life would teach their brothers and sisters all over the planet how to renew these ways and live in humility, having respect for all and a sense of oneness with each other and their Creator.

When the Elders of Saskatchewan established the Spiritual Unity of Tribes, they identified six prejudices affecting the "Nation of the Human." These are leadership, economic, racial, political, national, and religious prejudices. By meeting peacefully to understand these prejudices and the ways they have been detrimental to the welfare and progress of all humankind, the elders believe that this understanding will bring empowerment and the ability to advocate on behalf of all peoples, as well as eradication of these prejudices.

The gatherings aren't meant to be an answer unto themselves but are seen as a prototype of hope for the future, creating a caring and unifying standard and atmosphere. The spiritual com-

CEREMONIAL MASK, NUNIVAK ISLAND. E. S. Curtis, Special Collections Division, University of Washington Libraries, Negative No. NA 2006. _____

passion, tolerance, and equality that have been understood by native peoples for years are considered to be the foundation of these gatherings.

If one sits cross-legged across from Mary Stachelrodt and listens to her talk about her visions for the future, there is hope, a fierce hope backed by many deeds. And hope is a scarce and desperately needed commodity these days.

Clive Ponting of Wales, author of *The Green History of the World,* does not see much cause for hope. Based on the present use of fossil fuels,

deforestation, ozone depletion, and global warming, Ponting gives mankind just forty years before the earth will be rendered unlivable. Add choking pollution and limited food supplies to the fact that each year the world's population continues to explode, and Ponting predicts a series of environmental disasters and droughts, spreading famine, and epidemic plagues.

The last ecologically stable group of people to inhabit the earth, Ponting believes, were the hunters and gatherers such as the Inupiat and

PORTRAIT OF AN ESKIMO CHILD. *Duck-skin parka, buttontrimmed hat with fur ruff.* E. S. Curtis, PCA 49-15, Alaska State Library. _____

the Yupik. Yet he cautions that people can never return to that way of life, even if we so desire, because the earth cannot sustain millions of hunters and gatherers.

In the Bering Sea region, rapid assimilation into white society began around the turn of the century with the coming of the missionaries. Church-run, government-backed schools that sprang up along the coast did much to undermine the traditional ways of life. Children who were in school eight hours a day were not learning how to hunt and gather food with their families, nor were they able to shift locations with the seasons and the migratory animals they depended on for food and warmth.

Today, villages exercise far more local control, and efforts are under way to restructure education so that there is more language and culture curriculum incorporated into village schools. Some of the schools in the Bristol Bay and Bethel area are now teaching the first several grades in Yupik, with English as a second language. The program has been extremely successful.

In the past twenty years, promoting family and community wellness has taken on greater priority, and village councils are seizing responsibility to make those changes come about. Many communities have gone "dry" to the extent that every mail plane is greeted by an elder who checks luggage for alcohol. New regional alcohol- and drug-treatment centers are springing up in the bush that place a native emphasis on treating extended family locally.

There has also been a resurgence of interest in native stories and legends, traditional arts, and the coming together of youth with elders at spirit camps and youth conferences.

When Edward Curtis embarked on his final journey to Alaska in 1927, he fervently hoped that the white population would dwindle in the North and the country would be left alone. That didn't happen. But what he found among the Eskimo people—in their faces, their stories, their ceremonies, and their reverence toward everyday life—is a gift from the past that is still waiting to be received.

References

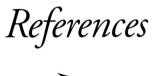

Allen, Arthur James. *A Whaler & Trader in the Arctic, 1895–1944: My Life with the Bowhead.* Anchorage, AK: Alaska Northwest Publishing Company, copyright 1978 by Alice Killbear.

Blair, William M. "Aid to Aborigines in Alaska Studied." *New York Times,* January 1, 1968.

Burroughs, John, John Muir, et al. *Alaska, The Harriman Expedition, 1899.* New York: Dover Publications, 1986.

Curtis, Edward S. *The North American Indian,* Vol. 20. Written, illustrated, and published by Curtis, with field research conducted under the patronage of J. Pierpont Morgan, Cambridge and Norwood, Massachusetts, 1930.

Curtis, Edward S. Log of the 1927 field season in northern Alaska. June Metcalfe Collection, 1905–1989. University of Fairbanks Archives Collection, The Elmer E. Rasmuson Library, Fairbanks, Alaska.

Curtis, Edward S. Papers, 1903–51; letters regarding his mining interests in Colfax, California, 1932–40, and his career as a photographer, 1932–51. Photostats of letters and documents regarding the publication of *The North American Indian,* 1903–35. Manuscripts and University Archives, University of Washington Libraries.

Curtis, Edward S. Photograph Collection Album 49, Alaska Historical Library. Twenty negatives made from original photogravure prints acquired by the Alaska State Museum of Eskimo portraits and village views, originally published in *The North American Indian* (Cambridge and Norwood, Massachusetts, 1907–1930).

Curtis, Edward S. Photographs from *The North American Indian* and published photographs from the souvenir albums from the Harriman Expedition of 1899. Special Collections Division, University of Washington Libraries.

Curtis, Edward S. "The Rush to the Klondike over the Mountain Passes." *The Century Illustrated,* March 1898.

Curtis, Edward S., with foreword and interview by Edward Marshall. "The Vanishing Redman." *Hampton Magazine,* May 1912.

Davis, Barbara A. *Edward S. Curtis: The Life and Times of a Shadow Catcher.* San Francisco, CA: Chronicle Books, 1985.

Fitzhugh, William W., and Susan A. Kaplan, with contributions by Henry B. Collins, Thomas Ager, Dorothy Jean Ray, and Saradell Ard Frederick. *Inua, Spirit World of the Bering Sea Eskimo.* Washington, DC: Smithsonian Institution Press, 1982.

Flury, James, and Lois Flury. *Edward S. Curtis' "The North American Indian": A Description of the Work, What Survives and Market Values.* Photo Reference File, Curtis, Edward S., University of Washington Libraries.

The Gathering V Newsletter, No. 1, March 1992. Duane Pierson, Treasurer, 1424 Turner Street, Fairbanks, AK 99701.

Gidley, Mick. "Edward Curtis Goes to the Mountain." *Pacific Northwest Quarterly,* October 1984.

Green, Paul, aided by Abbe Abbott. *I Am Eskimo, Aknik My Name.* Anchorage, AK: Alaska Northwest Books, 1959.

Hackett, Regina. "Exhibit May Dismay Edward Curtis Fans." *Seattle Post-Intelligencer,* August 10, 1989.

Harriman Photo Collection, 1899. Alaska and Polar Regions Department, Elmer E. Rasmuson Library, University of Alaska–Fairbanks.

Holm, Bill, and George Irving Quimby. *Edward S. Curtis in the Land of the War Canoes: A Pioneer Cinematographer in the Pacific Northwest,* 1980.

In the Spirit of the Family: Native Alcohol & Drug Counsellor's Family Systems Treatment Intervention Handbook. Calgary, AB: National Native Association of Treatment Directors, 1989.

Leinfeld, Judith, and Joseph Bloom. *A Long Way from Home: Effects of Public High Schools on Village Children Away from Home.* Center for Northern Educational Research and Institute of Social, Economic and Government Research, University of Alaska–Fairbanks.

Lindsey, Alton A. "The Harriman Alaska Expedition of 1899, Including the Identities of Those in the Staff Pictures." *Bioscience* 28, No. 6 (June 1978).

Lowry, Shannon. "The Dollmaker." *Alaska Magazine,* December 1989.

Lowry, Shannon. "The Magic of Masks." *Anchorage Times,* October 5, 1986.

Lyman, Christopher M. *The Vanishing Race and Other Illusions: Photographs of Indians by Edward S. Curtis.* New York: Pantheon, 1982.

Monroe, Robert D. "Seeing Edward Curtis and Beyond: The Iconography of the Harriman Expedition of 1899." *Northwest Photography,* December 1982.

Morgan, Murray. "The Grand Illusions of Edward S. Curtis." *The Northwest Book Review,* published by *The Weekly, Seattle's Newsmagazine,* May 1982.

Morris, Tim. "Untrained Anthropology." *Seattle Sun,* March 23, 1977.

Pratt, Kenneth L., and Robert D. Shaw. *A Petroglyphic Sculpture from Nunivak Island, Alaska. Contributions to the Anthropology of Southcentral and Southwestern Alaska.* Anthropological Papers of the University of Alaska 24 (1 & 2). In press.

Ray, Dorothy Jean. *The Eskimos of Bering Strait, 1650–1898.* Seattle: University of Washington Press, 1975. Reprint, 1992.

Richards, Thomas, Jr. "Claims Bill Sails Through." *Tundra Times,* December 17, 1971.

Selkinghaus, Jessie A. "The Curtis Indian Pictures." *American Magazine of Art,* October 1925.

Senungetuk, Vivian, and Paul Tiulana. *A Place for Winter: Paul Tiulana's Story.* Anchorage, AK: CIRI Foundation, 1987.

Tarzan, Delores. "Shadowy Evidence: The Photography of Edward S. Curtis." *Seattle Times/Seattle Post-Intelligencer,* August 13, 1989.

Thornton, Gene. "Why Is Curtis Unknown?" *New York Times,* October 17, 1971.

Weaver, Howard. "Nixon Set to Sign Pipeline Bill." *Anchorage Daily News,* November 16, 1973.